TRUSTEES
IN HIGHER EDUCATION

TRUSTEES
IN HIGHER EDUCATION

Their Functions and Coordination

BY GERALD P. BURNS

President, INDEPENDENT COLLEGE FUNDS OF AMERICA, INC.

CONTENTS

FOREWORD

Now that the role of the regent and trustee in the institution of higher learning is taking on added significance, it is good to see a person with the qualifications of Gerald P. Burns write another book on universities, colleges and their governing boards.

Dr. Burns is uniquely qualified to write on the trusteeship because of his intensive study of it throughout the United States and abroad—a study spanning two decades. He presents this work in both scholarly and business-like form, perhaps because he is both a scholar (with *two* earned doctorates) and an educational executive (president of a federation of more than 500 colleges). In his professional career he bridges the financial gap between colleges and corporations in a manner not unlike the typical trustee or regent.

The book successfully combines the wisdom of some of the nation's great trustees by reiterating the best of traditional procedures and offering exciting new departures proven valuable in recent experimentation.

In terms of form, the volume is skillfully organized with chapters arranged in logical progression for complete reading or occasional reference. It is also written in brief and straightforward language without resorting to educational cliches or academic rhetoric. In terms of content, it provides a comprehensive overview of the entire field of governance in higher education and it deals specifically with solutions to the major problems which inevitably confront boards of regents and trustees.

Because of its penetrating analyses and illuminating judgments this coverage offers a refreshing and significant treatment of the trusteeship.

Roy Rowe, *Past President*
Association of Governing Boards
Washington, D. C.

INTRODUCTION

The role of the trustee or regent in higher education is dynamic and important. These men (and women) serve on boards, councils and committees to establish policy for colleges and universities. This volume examines their service, reporting on past performances, analyzing current activities, and suggesting future functions. It is designed to answer some of the questions and solve some of the problems confronting these board members. It will, also, clarify duties and responsibilities so that administrators, faculty, students and others genuinely interested in higher education will understand the developing role of the trustee.

In comparison with the importance of the trusteeship (or regency), relatively little has been written about it. Recently there has been renewed research and writing on the functions of board members, but much more is needed. As late as 1947, Professor George Counts said there were all too few studies of "that uniquely American institution, the lay board of trustees." The board, which links the university to society, must help bridge that gap and have the last word on matters of major policy. The profound changes occurring in our society, the exciting explosion of knowledge, and the enormous expansion of higher education, make it imperative that trustees and administrators understand fully the problems and potentialities involved in board membership.

This study presents in logical sequence the history, current status, and future possibilities of the trusteeship. It describes the scope of higher education, its governance, its administration, and the specific responsibilities of board members. It concludes with some speculation about the future of the trusteeship and higher education.

Higher education is the stage and professional educators the supporting players in this presentation, but the trustees are the stars. The contents will acquaint the new trustee with his responsibilities and remind the veteran trustee of his opportunities. To the majority of the devoted, hard-working board members of colleges and universities across the nation, this book should prove reassuring, and it may serve to rekindle the enthusiasm of those few who have tired of their task.

In addition to aiding the trustees and other intra-mural persons, this book should be helpful to many persons outside of the ivied halls. It may assist foundation officers, corporate executives, interested alumni, and other friends (and critics) of higher education in understanding the methods of policy formulation in colleges and universities.

The book's basic objective is to help trustees perform more expertly their roles as board members. I believe that if properly selected, oriented and serviced, trustees will function more industriously and productively, and also will find interesting and enjoyable their relationship to academic institutions.

My philosophy about boards of trustees may be stated by paraphrasing Clemenceau: Education is too important to be left entirely to the faculty and administration. Outside, objective, detached perspectives are needed in any major undertaking, and the operation of a college is no ex-

ception. Such perspectives derive from knowledgeable
sympathetic, intelligent, voluntary leaders in the community.

There is no single source of knowledge on or specific
method of determining how to select, recruit, and orient
such lay leaders. What follows in this book is based upon
three major sources. First, the careful perusal of previous
writing and research in this area. Second, the detailed discussion of their trusteeship experience with distinguished
board members. Third, my own personal research, training
and experience.

There have been several studies of the trusteeship made
and published during the past decade. Attention is invited
to those documented after each chapter and especially,
to those annotated in Appendix A.

On the second source, many knowledgeable college trustees provided valuable contributions to this study. A partial listing of those who contributed most significantly is
provided in Appendix B.

On the third source, the importance of the role of college
trustees was brought forcefully to my attention in 1952 by
Chancellor Henry T. Heald of New York University. During three years of service as an administrative officer working with the N. Y. U. Board for Development, it became
obvious that these lay leaders could, if properly organized,
oriented and stimulated, exert a profound influence on the
future of the institution.

Subsequently I was elected Vice President of Reed College and assisted in reorganizing the administration of the
college and strengthening its Board of Trustees. In addition, a major project was undertaken in cooperation with
the University of Oregon that resulted in my giving several

lectures, publishing certain articles and directing a regional conference—all on the subject of the orientation and training of college trustees.

More recently, in lecturing and in teaching seminars in the administration of higher education at Teachers College, Portland State College, New York University and Rutgers University, this subject of the trusteeship was further explored in depth. In the summer of 1960, a Ford Foundation grant was accepted and a study made of the governance and financing of higher education in Western Europe. In the summer of 1962, a Sloan Foundation grant was accepted and a study made on governance and financing of higher education in the Orient and Southeast Asia.

Finally, the privilege of working closely with the sixty trustees of the Independent College Funds of America deserves mention. This national board is composed of college presidents, association directors, and business leaders. The latter group provided specific insights on how corporation executives at the highest echelons can serve most effectively as college trustees. (See Appendix B)

If there are already several books on the trusteeship, why yet another? This is a sound question worthy of a straight answer. The majority of the earlier publications in this field were written by a single person. While some of these authors were perceptive and eloquent, while some of these books make significant contributions, all are open to the criticism that they represent a single viewpoint or philosophy.

This volume, although written by a single author, is essentially a *consensus of several viewpoints* or philosophies, the common threads of their different fabrics having been synthesized herein. The distinguished trustees who collaborated informally in this book deserve primary credit for the enlightened perspectives here for the first time clearly enunciated. No single individual can comprehend all facets of an assignment as vast and variable as the trusteeship. For that reason, several were brought actively into this study; several others were brought in by virtue of sharing generously, if unofficially, their views on this subject.

As a final statement of scope, it must be mentioned that no one book can cover all the details of a field as intangible and diverse as collegiate governance. Similarly, no single chapter can encompass all aspects of a topic as profound as the evolution of the trusteeship or as expansive as the current status of higher education. This presentation, therefore, should be considered a succinct over-view of the subject of the trusteeship; those wishing more details on any facet may turn to other books and articles, especially publications mentioned in the *documentation and commentary* after each chapter.

I wish to thank most sincerely the lay trustees and professional educators, without whose inspiration, encouragement, and assistance this project could not have been completed. However, I take full responsibility for any heresies, ambiguities, or factual errors occurring herein. I wish, also, to thank the trustees of the United States Steel Foundation for its grant toward the publishing costs of this project.

G. P. B.

TRUSTEES
IN HIGHER EDUCATION

1 EVOLUTION OF THE TRUSTEESHIP

The majority of our contemporary social, civic and educational issues have their origins or roots far back in history. When the evolution of these issues or movements is blithely passed over, the underlying reasons for their current existence and their future direction may be lost. Aristotle's wisdom "He who considers things in their growth and origin will obtain the clearest view of them," and Lincoln's advice "We cannot escape history," have the sagacity of the ages behind them.

This analysis of the antecedents of academic lay-leadership is brief and limited. It deals with those historical events of importance to present day operations. It emphasizes those ideas and events that are adjudged to form the basis upon which the foundations of successful governance and administration may rest.

ORIGINS OF GOVERNANCE

Medievalists hold that the true university (of several disciplines, faculties, degrees, and ceremonies) was produced by the Middle Ages, but ancient history indicates that the function of higher education goes back at least to the 4th Century B.C.

With respect to the word "university," Rashdall claims it is misleading to apply the name to the schools of ancient Athens and Alexandria.[1] It was not until the twelfth and thirteenth centuries that there emerged in the world institutions with those features of higher education which we now technically identify with a university. Functionally, these later universities may have been similar to their precursors of the ancient world since they still stressed investigation and instruction. Structurally, they were different from the earlier schools in that they developed new patterns of control and organization.

The Academy of Plato (387 B.C.), and the Lyceum of Aristotle (335 B.C.), the Museum at Alexandria (332 B.C.), and the *madaris* of the Islamic world influenced the later institutions of higher education on an operational level. However, they were not corporate structures like the medieval universities of centuries later. These early schools had no trustees and only a single administrator or *scholarch* to direct the institution and handle its endowment.

Historians usually limit the term "Middle Ages" to Western Europe, and hence they pay little attention to the contributions made to higher education by the Byzantine Empire and the Islamic world. Constantine the Great, Justinian I, and Basil I, developed a variety of higher institutions which today would be called universities. These helped to keep alive much of the Hellenistic traditions and knowledge which, in later centuries, were partially incorporated in the European universities. Governance of these early institutions resided primarily in the state and the municipality.[2]

Islamic learning triggered the maturation of higher education to the point where some scholars feel that the emergence of the European universities as quality institutions was dependent upon their Islamic antecedents. The four major institutions of the Mohammedans prior to 100 B.C. were Bail al-Hikmah, Cordova, al-Azhar and Dar al-Hikmah. The curriculum of these institutions leaned more toward the humanistic than the scientific. Although some research was conducted, instruction was their primary function.

In terms of administration, the larger schools had principals who appointed the faculty subject to the patron's approval. While the state was essentially the sponsor of the Byzantian universities, the individual rulers (caliphs or sultans) were the patrons of the Islamic institution. The teachers themselves, rather than the institutions, awarded the diplomas.

In terms of governance, institutional trustees as such were non-existent since the external patronship was all-powerful. The patrons controlled the universities by appointing the principals and approving the principals' employment of instructors.

As the Western European universities were founded, they embraced many of the curricular forms of the earlier institutions, but they added an important new dimension of structure, namely the concept of corporation or social organism. Expanded trade, the crusades, new technology, the revival of Roman Law, developments in medicine, the

availability of Aristotle's Works and an increase in secondary education were instrumental in bringing about the
establishment of higher institutions in Italy, France, Ger-
many and England.

The new universities in Europe offered work in both
general and specialized education. In the northern universities, most of the professors were in holy orders; in the
Italian universities, most of the faculty members were laymen. In the south, the municipalities supported the universities, whereas in the north, the state and the church
were the patrons.[3] In France a powerful struggle developed
between the state and the church, each seeking to be the
dominant patron. From the controversy developed the concept of universities being autonomous structures and as
such independent of both church and state. In the Italian
universities the students employed the teachers and retained control until the 15th century, at which point the
municipal authorities assumed leadership through bodies
similar to modern American boards of trustees. This appears to be the earliest instance of what is now termed the
trusteeship. The northern universities, with the exception
of Leyden and St. Andrews, maintained faculty control
of the institutions.

The Medieval period was followed by the Renaissance
period which witnessed the establishment of many of the
world's greatest centers of higher learning. Included in
this group are such institutions as Bologna, Paris, Oxford
and Cambridge. Instruction continued as the dominant
function, with investigation consisting more of conceptual
than factual activity.

Brubacher and Rudy observe, "Since medieval times the
tradition in European colleges and universities has been

one of self-government. Masters had banded together and governed themselves in the manner of the guilds."[4] This self-government, with some modification, has continued to the present. The modification is largely legalistic, rather than an actual change in the power structure of the institution.

During this period, European institutions received support from the church; in consequence of this, representatives of the church were appointed to oversee the expenditures of the universities. However, in those early days and extending up to the present, the representatives actually exercised a very limited amount of authority and served more as advisors than trustees. Later, the Crown and private benefactors were the sources of support and control.

EARLY INSTITUTIONS IN AMERICA

American colleges and universities carried over some of the European historical traditions. However, the usually passive role of governing boards in Europe was not followed in this country except in a few institutions. William and Mary was one such exception, where the tradition of a self-governing faculty was maintained for many years after its founding.[5]

The celebrated Dartmouth College Case, where the college president and state legislators opposed the board of trustees on the fundamental issue of college control (and lost), confirmed the dominant role of the college trustee in American higher education.[6]

One of the main reasons advanced for the strength of boards of control in early American institutions was the absence of numerous, experienced, well-educated faculty members; a situation without parallel in Europe. Moreover,

the early colleges and universities in the colonies were
closely related to their communities and the local church;
in Europe there was a cosmopolitan quality which defied
close lay control (with the possible exception of the Italian
universities).

Kirkpatrick underscores this contention in holding that
the American college presidency is a unique office and that
it arrived with that other peculiar American institution, the
lay board of governors. This latter was a device of the in-
ventive frontiersman during colonial days and it has per-
sisted across the continent for more than two centuries.[7]
This colonial period began with the founding of Harvard
in 1636 and might be concluded with the adoption of the
Constitution in 1789. Other colleges established in this period were Yale, Brown, Dartmouth, Pennsylvania, Princeton, Columbia, Rutgers and William and Mary.

In the early institutions, the majority of the trustees were
men of of the cloth. There were many reasons for ministers
serving on these college boards. First, the clerics were frequently the best educated men in the community. Second,
these churchmen provided valuable professional guidance,
since one of the primary purposes of the early colleges was
to train ministers. Third, as leaders in the communities, the
men of God offered a logical link between the college, the
church and the community.

It is interesting to note that some of the same reasons
prevail today for the emphasis on having business and industrial leaders as trustees and regents. Businessmen are
generally among the best educated men in the community.
These industrialists provide broad-based guidance on
what kind of educated manpower is most needed. As
leaders in their communities, these executives are logisti-

cally situated to offer both financial and moral support as natural links between "town and gown."

In Colonial days, the collegiate boards had few (if any) members from the distaff side. Here again, there were logical reasons for this. Women students were seldom seen in the early institutions; universal suffrage had not arrived and "a woman's place was in the home"; the European universities had no female board members, so it was reasoned that the American colleges didn't need them.

This aversion to women trustees and regents continued for a century. It is reasonable to assume that men's colleges can get along without females on their governing boards. However, it is difficult to justify their having been left off the boards of co-educational institutions—especially great urban universities—until the twentieth century. Indeed, it was not until 1965 that New York University installed two women (Mrs. Albert Lasker and Mrs. Vincent Astor) on its board of trustees.

Although the early Colonial colleges were established and supported generally by religious sects, partial responsibility for governance and financing was assumed by the state (colony). In effect the church, the state, *and* the general public has a vested interest in their welfare. Thus, it should come as no surprise when historians report that boards of trustees were formed at the founding of the colonial colleges (*e.g.*, the Harvard Corporation) and legal control has rested with them ever since.

THE PERIOD OF EXPANSION

The development of higher education in the United States might have been very different if Continental rather than English university traditions had been dominant. The

English universities began, by the time of the Renaissance, to change into loosely federated associations of residential colleges. The Continental universities, on the contrary, were becoming non-resident graduate schools offering various kinds of post-baccalaureate training. One common bond existing among all three (English, Continental, and American) types of universities was the governance by groups of trustees. Although it appears that European institutions generally developed bodies with the title of Boards, it was left to the young American institutions to present the real justification for (and subsequent establishment of) true college Boards of Trustees.

The need for these functionaries in American higher education, as implied earlier, resided in three factors; necessity for lay administrative leadership; intimate relationship with the local church and community for personnel and funds, prompting close lay financial leadership; lack of the existence of the scholarly guild which caused a vacuum in top management, calling for lay policy leadership. In referring to the initial reasons for external assistance and objective guidance in the early colleges and universities, Harvard's James Conant says, "The history of universities—in truth, of all human institutions, lay or clerical—proves by melancholy experience, that seminaries founded for the common weal, in the furtherance of sound knowledge, are, if left to themselves without an external and vigilant, and intelligent and disinterested supervision, regularly deflected from the great end for which they were created, and perverted to the private advantages of those through whom that end, it was confidently hoped, would be best accomplished."[8]

The need for trustees has been continually validated throughout the history of American higher education. It is not difficult to trace this need (and how it was met) as the basis for the now reasonably well-defined role of the trustees in our colleges and universities.

The lay boards in colonial colleges were of many types and most of them exercised full control with the president serving as a member of the board. Generally, the trustees were clergymen, college graduates and men of stature in the community.[9]

THE PERIOD OF DEVELOPMENT

It was during this period that the distinguishing characteristics of American higher education developed. Guided by strong lay leadership, and a rapidly developing professional professorial group, the colleges and universities began to evolve the basic concept of our American system of higher education.[10] This concept stresses the necessity for effective teaching being the first responsibility of the college; that the search for truth is fundamental; that higher education should be both residential and non-residential; that men and women, rich and poor, young and old, should be educated to their maximum capacities; that there shall be both publicly and privately supported institutions; that all institutions shall be free of government control after being chartered by their respective states; and that lay boards of trustees shall guide them.

The majority of the privately-supported colleges were church-related. This was an outgrowth of the fact that their first function was to train ministers. Indeed, as Hofstadter observes, "With the development of Princeton, we have the characteristic pattern for American private college government; control through a unitary board of non-resident, non-academic persons; the presence on the board of clergymen either in equal numbers to laymen or in predominant strength; a denominational affiliation of some kind, but hospitality to matriculants of other sects; the centrality in the institution's governance and development of the strong president; the essential independence, despite the occasional presence of state officials on boards of control, from either control or support by the state."[11]

Following the Civil War, a tremendous growth occurred in the number of higher institutions being founded. At the same time, there was greatly increased participation of faculties in academic government. This interesting development was particuluarly apparent at Harvard where in 1863 the faculty "organized" on a basis similar to faculties of today.[12] They adopted the title of Academic Council but limited their activities in administration to several public lectures. However, in the following years the Council acquired considerably more power over academic arrangements. The two publicly-authorized governing boards of Harvard did not relinquish their final authority and responsibility for educational policy, but they did delegate large blocks of power to the faculties.[13]

THE PERIOD OF STABILITY

Some changes have occurred in the historical or traditional role of the trustee since 1900. These were primarily concerned with granting more power to the faculty. In addition, boards recognized the necessity for expanding their own committee functions because of the growing size and complexity of their individual institutions. The patterns of board functions established in the colonial colleges and developed during the ensuing 200 years began to achieve a degree of stability.

During this period of rapid expansion in enrollment, another more important change was taking place. The financial condition of all private (and many public) colleges and universities was deteriorating.[14] This situation was caused by a combination of factors, chief among which were: first, prices were spiralling upward rapidly; second, inflation crept in after the great depression and ran wild after World War II; third, tuition charges were unrealistically low causing each new enrollee to become an added liability; fourth, faculty salaries were so inadequate that the best men (especially in the sciences) were leaving for jobs in government and industry; fifth, collegiate plant maintenance and expansion had been minimal because of the three wars and campuses had deteriorated.

Because of this dismal situation, educational and civic leaders were shocked into action. They recognized that the students, faculty and administration could not cope with these monumental problems. They saw that the aged, inert and honorific trustees were not helping. The situation called for deeds, rather than words. Fortunately, the American people, lay and professional, evinced genuine concern for this situation and took action to correct it. During the first half of the twentieth century, corporations, foundations, and individuals gave generously of their time, talent and funds to help higher education. There was a rebirth of interest and effort on the part of lay boards in both private and public institutions to advance and improve the position of their colleges and universities both financially and academically.

It was at the end of this first fifty years that Ordway Tead summarized the task of trustees as follows:

Trustees are, of course, in the last analysis, holding the operation of education *in trust as a public service.* Every college has now become in fact a public agency; and it is required to gain and hold public confidence. To do this means a two-way relationship and trust. The wider public has to realize that for it to perform its unique mission the college has to have its own special degree of freedom, of elbow room, of leisure, and of absence of influence from outside pressures.

And on the other hand the college in its turn, while being protected in its internal autonomy, has to exercise its responsibility to assure the best possible utilization of its resources of men, ideas and money. We should never forget also that one vital aspect of that responsibility is the assertion of the rightful interest of the university and college in that which may be *new,* which may as yet be *unsaid,* and which may be thus far *untried* in the intellectual and spiritual realm. For the college is democracy's institution uniquely charged to be the custodian of truth seeking and truth affirming.

It can be a noble public service to act as the trustee of an institution of higher learning.[15]

During this period, many students of administration and several knowledgeable trustees said that, in addition to strengthening the board with more able and active trustees, two other steps should be taken: first, expand and extend the power of the president to cope with the growing complexities of the larger institutions;[16] and, second, utilize the methods and techniques of major business corporations where they are applicable to higher education. They point out that the arrangement of college management closely resembles that of an American business or industrial corporation.[17] The president, as general manager, administers the affairs of the institution under broad policies officially approved not by the faculty, but by his board. While it seems logical that the trustees should pass on the major policies of the institution, the faculty should have an important role in assisting the president with the formulation of these policies, especially when they relate directly to educational issues.

Some of this recommended action, and other new departures were accepted and incorporated into the operations of many institutions. New York University and Reed College supply two classic illustrations. Both of these institutions effected major self-studies and reconstituted their governing boards. Unfortunately, many institutions ignored the need for change, did not alter their out-dated methods, failed to improve their boards, and in general did little to meet the challenge. The upshot of the situation is that as we move into the last half of the twentieth century, we find all institutions in need of greater financial support and in many the need is critical.

THE CHANGING ROLE IN HISTORY

If one summarized the historical role of the trustee as defined in most American institutions of higher education at this time, it might appear as follows: hold the charter of the institution, establish the over-all policies, select the chief executive officer, raise funds, approve the budget, and represent the institution with its publics.

The broad authority and general delineation of power residing in college and university boards caused Chancellor Capen of the University of Buffalo to say they constitute a "Simon pure example of authoritarian government."[18] Rauh observes, "In most cases the enabling charter or legislation gives the board full power to manage the institution."[19] Ruml points out that final authority and responsibility is

CHRONOLOGY OF INSTITUTIONS AND
THEIR GOVERNANCE

Period	Typical Institutions	Typical Governance
Origins: Europe Asia Africa	Plato's Academy Byzantian Universities Universities of Bologna, Paris, Oxford, Cambridge.	Representatives of the state, the church, and wealthy patrons. Some student governance due to employment of faculty. Considerable self-governance.
Early American	Harvard, Yale, Dartmouth, Brown, Princeton and other colleges and universities.	Representatives of the church and the colony (community). Heavy emphasis on clergy.
Expansion	Union, St. John's, other liberal arts colleges. Expansion of professional and graduate schools.	Representatives of the public at large. Emphasis on community leaders and wealthy patrons.
Development	Land grant colleges and universities. Development of state teachers colleges and private urban universities.	Representatives of the public at large. Emphasis on community leaders and business executives.
Stability	Stabilizing status of land grant and state teachers colleges. The advent of the "multiversity" and its modification into "cluster colleges".	Representatives of the public at large. Emphasis on persons who would provide "work, wealth and wisdom".

that of the trustees, and, "they may abdicate from their position of authority, but they cannot annul it; they may vacate their posts, but they cannot destroy them; they may delegate activities and decision, but they cannot thereby avoid their own responsibilities."[20] These statements indicate that although this considerable power and authority is little understood and seldom used, it still exists and could be a vital factor in strengthening and improving the operations of countless institutions.

DOCUMENTATION AND COMMENTARY

[1] Hastings Rashdall, *The Universities of Europe in the Middle Ages*, 1936 edition, Oxford: Clarendon Press, Vol. II, p. 458.

[2] *Ibid.*, p. 186.

[3] *Ibid.*, p. 189.

[4] John S. Brubacher and Willis Rudy, *Higher Education in Transition*, New York: Harper, 1958, p. 26.

[5] Brubacher and Rudy, *op. cit.*, p. 27.

[6] L. B. Richardson, *History of Dartmouth College*, Hanover: Dartmouth College Publications, 1932, Vol. I, Chap. 6.

[7] J. E. Kirkpatrick, *The American College and Its Rulers*, New York: New Republic, Inc., 1926, p. 299.

[8] James B. Conant, *Academical Patronage and Superintendence*, Cambridge: Harvard University, 1953, p. 37.

[9] Brubacher and Rudy, *op. cit.*, p. 30.

[10] Brubacher and Ruby, *op. cit.*, p. 28.

[11] Richard Hofstadter and Walter P. Metzger, *The Development of Academic Freedom In the United States*, New York: Columbia University Press, 1955, p. 143.

[12] W. H. Cowley, "The Government and Administration of Higher Education: Whence and Whither?", *Journal of the American Association of Collegiate Registrars*, July, 1947, Vol. 22, No. 4, p. 477.

[13] According to publications of the Harvard Corporation and the Board of Overseers.

[14] Philip H. Coombs, "An Economist's View of Higher Education". Dexter M. Keezer, Editor, *Financing Higher Education 1960-1970*, New York, McGraw-Hill Book Company, Inc. 1959, p. 21.

[15] Ordway Tead, *Trustees, Teachers, Students—Their Role in Higher Education*, Univ. of Utah Press: Salt Lake City, 1951, pp. 23-24.

[16] Gerald P. Burns, "Needed: Presidents With Authority", *College and University Business*, Vol. 31, No. 3, September, 1961.

[17] Tyrus Hillway, "How Trustees Judge a College President," *School and Society*, Vol. 89, Number 2186, Feb. 11, 1961, p. 51.

[18] Samuel P. Capen, *The Management of Universities*, Buffalo: Steward Publishing Co., 1953, p. 93.

[19] Morton A. Rauh, *College and University Trusteeship*, Yellow Springs, Ohio: The Antioch Press, 1959, p. 13.

[20] Beardsley Ruml and Donald H. Morrison, *Memo to a College Trustee*, New York: McGraw-Hill, 1959, pp. 3-4.

2 CURRENT SCOPE AND STATUS OF HIGHER EDUCATION

Building upon the evolutionary aspects of goverance, this chapter presents an overview of the scope and status of higher education. Although the trustee will function primarily on an intramural basis, an acquaintance with the total area of operation should prove helpful.

THE "ESTABLISHMENT" IN HIGHER EDUCATION

Higher education is composed of all post-high school institutions of learning. These include junior and senior colleges, undergraduate and graduate schools, liberal arts and professional institutions. The United States Office of Education lists more than 2,000 separate institutions in these several categories.

Within the above categories are many kinds and varieties of schools. Indeed the word "school" is often used interchangeably with institution, college or university. However, as a general rule in higher education, a *school* or *college* is a single unit, whereas a *university* is composed of two or more such units.

Another difference is in the method of support. Approximately 1,200 institutions of higher education are primarily privately supported; and about 800 are largely publicly-supported. Few if any derive all their support from either source. A considerable blending of support has occurred in recent years.

Governance and control are usually related to the type of support. In public institutions, the boards are frequently appointed by the chief executive of the (tax) supporting area. In private institutions, the boards are usually self-perpetuating in whole or in part.

POTENTIALITIES AND PROBLEMS

The current scope and status of American higher education can best be presented in terms of the major problems and potentialities facing the field. Those considered potentialities are positive, and among the more important are public interpretation, curriculum revision, extra-curricular possibilities and competition with other institutions. Those considered problems are negative, and among the more important are financial hazards, government influence, personnel shortages, and enrollment problems.

It may have been fortunate that the Russians put a man in orbit before the United States, because it caused a much-needed awakening to the fact that we were not doing all that might be done in the related fields of science and education. All at once attention was focused on the technological achievements of the U.S.S.R., which many had considered a sleeping giant or a nation of wild-eyed revolutionaries. Investigation indicates that these technological achievements came about through extensive education and rigorous training—perhaps more and better in certain aspects than are provided in this country.[1]

After the initial surprise of the Russian advances began to dim, so too did the interest of the great majority of Americans in the scientific and educational status of this nation. However, many thoughtful leaders realized that even though the early concern had faded, the point had been scored; that a hard look at our schools and colleges should be taken. As this hard look was taken, it became apparent that the Russians were not so far ahead, that they were leading in specific areas only, and that from the broad view of incorporating humanistic education along with scientific training, the American educational system was the best for the attainment of our national goals.

As the observations were made, as data were gathered, as conclusions were drawn, it also became apparent that, although American schools and colleges were doing a creditable job, they could be improved. Some justifiable criticism (and much unjustifiable criticism) was levelled at the educators, especially those in higher education. The main burden of the constructive criticism was that education in the United States was not changing fast enough to keep up with the shrinking globe, the jet age, or the era of the atom. In an effort to make the appropriate changes, to correct the deficiencies and to enhance the strong points, it became obvious that the above-mentioned potentialities and problems provided the stimulus needed and the guidelines desired to get on with the job most efficiently.

PUBLIC INTERPRETATION

Public interpretation of higher education has taken on new importance. Educators realize now more than ever that they and their institutions are not separate and apart from the community, but rather, are related to and provide services for the community, thus giving rise to this new emphasis on public relations.

Schoenfeld has outlined the essence of the public interpretation function for American higher education:

1. Improved public relations is needed as never before if our schools are to continue to merit and receive adequate support.
2. Public relations correctly conceived is no bag of publicity tricks; it is inextricably linked with sound administration in all its aspects.
3. Public relations is not the job of a single individual; every contact between the university and its constituency is an episode in the complex flow of institutional relationships.[2]

These principles apply not alone to the private institution dependent upon voluntary support, but to the tax-supported institution as well. It is imperative for the president of a state-supported institution to accept the principle that the college over which he presides is *of, for* and *by the people* and that it is their desires which must determine the amount and nature of support which the institution will receive.[3] Since all tax-payers support the public institutions, these colleges and universities must be more sensitive and responsive to the people than the privately-supported institutions.

Whether a college or university is publicly supported or privately supported, ultimately its support comes from the people. To insure a continuance of support, it is necessary to interpret adequately the services of the institution to the public. Obviously, the general public is composed of several segments with different relationships to the institution. There are the legislators, trustees, alumni, donors, prospects, parents of students and potential students. And, internally, there are the students, faculty, and administration. Because of these different publics, and the variety of media and techniques used to contact them, the job of interpreting has become difficult and important, calling for skilled, professional workers. Then, too, since educational institutions are all desirous of doing the best possible interpretive job (in order to attract outstanding high school students and to activate generous donors) some competition inevitably occurs.

The vital point is that the American public has become interested in education. Action has been taken on the local, state and national levels to improve and expand our educational programs. This kind of interest and action is highly salutary, and institutions must answer honestly and accurately the questions the public is raising. Higher education should actually lead public opinion, not just be responsive to it.

CURRICULUM REVISION

Curriculum revision is one of the most important challenges facing higher education today. The various fields of knowledge are burgeoning with such rapidity that all educational institutions must make special efforts to stay abreast. No college or university can rest on past performance. Advances in specialized fields such as electronics, atomic power and automation require that higher institutions accept primary responsibility for training young people for leadership in these new and expanding areas.

In addition to the advances in scientific and technological subject matter, significant strides have been made in the social and political sciences. Man's world is smaller now, and he must learn to live in peace with other men if he is to live at all. These advances must be incorporated into the curriculum. Trustees as leaders in the larger community can and should help bring about this incorporation. In the long run the aims of higher education will be best served if the trustees understand and exercise their proper supervisory functions in academic affairs.[4] This includes their asking for facts and figures regarding the size of classes, and the range of departmental offerings which indicate whether or not the instructional program is consistent with the declared purposes of the institution. The trustees should then work cooperatively with the president and the faculty in initiating such modifications in program as seem desirable to all concerned. This procedure continues the traditional faculty influence in educational policy and practice, but it assures appropriate objective action. It may even eliminate the intolerable delays which sometimes afflict academic bodies.

Along with the new knowledge discovered in the subject fields or scholarly disciplines, research has uncovered valuable techniques bearing upon human relations and communications. For example, in public relations, in communications, and in new teaching methods, the innumerable unique dimensions of television, utilized in both the home and the school, indicate that curriculum revision is desirable. Despite the extraordinary increase in man's knowledge aggregated in recent years, sound academic offerings, superior teaching and technical innovations can bring about a reduction in the time students must remain with the institution. In addition, better articulation between high school and college curriculum will prove valuable.

Considerable resistance has been brought to bear on those attempting to tamper with the curriculum. Vested academic interests make revision and innovation difficult to the point where many presidents, deans and trustees have nearly given up trying to effect change and modification in this area. Other aspects of this problem, and suggested methods of meeting it, are examined in subsequent chapters.

EXTRA-CURRICULAR POSSIBILITIES

Extra-curricular possibilities provide other challenges for higher education. For many years, sports and social events comprising the bulk of the extra-curricular offerings were thought of as not really educational. They were considered rather relaxing diversionary pursuits for the students. During the last few years, however, it has been proven that well-planned and executed extra-curricular programs can have beneficial educational, cultural and physical effects.

The classroom or laboratory is not the only place on campus where learning takes place. Indeed, it appears from the experiments at Reed College that more quantitative and qualitative learning takes place in the extra-curricular programs than was realized earlier. Considering how little time is spent in actual lectures, laboratories and conferences, it is logical to expect that all the other waking hours will contribute to the purpose for which a student attends college—

to grow in spirit, mind and body. Sometimes student conversation is more important than organized activities.

As more trustees and educators realize what an unusual opportunity or challenge is offered higher education to do a better humanistic job through the extra-curricular program, colleges and universities will invest more time and money in this expanding area. Traditional forms, such as sports, student government and social events, are being evaluated and improved; newer forms, such as student publications, independent study and foreign travel are gaining in popularity.

One of the newest and most promising developments in this area is student participation in co-curricular, as well as extra-curricular matters. A few of the more interesting concepts behind this theory of student participation are enumerated by Henderson as follows:

1. The giving of some measure of responsibility to students will result in getting a response from them. Furthermore, the ability to carry responsibility is a type of skill, and the skill should be acquired when the young person is developing rapidly, intellectually and otherwise.

2. The theory, then, of inviting student participation is that these problems will be better solved if the students have some voice in solving them because they have a better knowledge as to the nature of the problems and have ideas as to their solutions. Furthermore this participation will be more apt to assure responsible action on their part in carrying through decisions that are made.

3. They also have ideas about their needs, and to the extent that their motivations can be harnessed, the educational job will be better done. College professors sometimes resist the participation of the students in making evaluations of the results of teaching; and in some respects, such as in judging

the professional qualifications of the faculty member, the students are not the best judges. But they are the recipients of the lectures given in the classroom or of the discussions and experiences that take place, and they can make appraisals of the effectiveness of many of these teaching efforts. Thus the participation of students, either through the direction of the teacher himself or of some organized effort through student government, in evaluations of teaching effectiveness may result in improvements in the teaching.[5]

Based upon Henderson's comments, the Reed College experience, and the studies by Sanford at Vassar, it is reasonable to anticipate that trustees, administrators, faculty members and students may evince greater interest in the co-curricular and extra-curricular programs in the years ahead.[6]

INSTITUTIONAL COMPETITION

Institutional competition is providing a real challenge in higher education today. This is a desirable situation in that this kind of challenge places renewed emphasis on admissions officers seeking highly qualified students. The standards of all our colleges and universities are elevated when they are striving for academic excellence. Educational competition in certain areas promotes this.

There are many kinds of institutions making up our dual system of public and private higher education in America. The public institutions are tax supported, usually by the city or the state. The private institutions are tuition and gift supported and usually receive some income from endowment. Within the public group are the municipal colleges, community colleges, teachers colleges and state universities with their many professional schools and state-wide services. Within the private group are junior colleges, technical institutions, liberal arts colleges, and great universities— some with church relationships, some with no denominational connections.

Each college and university in this nation is a little different from the other. The diversity in aims and outcomes gives a rich and varied flavor to the education and training of the persons graduating from these institutions. Since each is in some degree competing with the other for the brighter student, talented teacher, and able researcher, friendly rivalry and mild competition promotes continued striving for academic excellence.

FINANCIAL HAZARDS

Educational institutions have in the past operated in a deficit position—they have never charged what their services cost. Consequently, as enrollments increased, the deficits grew proportionately larger. And this financial pinch was felt by the public (tax-supported) as well as the private (tuition and gift-supported) institutions.

It is estimated by the United States Office of Education that the gift income of all institutions of higher education totalled $1.45 billion in 1963.[7] During 1963 there was a total enrollment of 4,800,000 students and total expenditures of $9.02 billion. Of this total, $5.1 billion was in public, and $3.9 billion in private funds. Private institutions received about 80 per cent of all gifts and grants. Legislatures continue to augment their appropriations to public institutions despite increasing income from student fees, foundation grants and voluntary gifts.

Later chapters will examine in detail various facets of this problem of finance. Its over-riding importance, in both public and private colleges and universities, qualifies it as one deserving the careful attention of all leaders in higher education.

GOVERNMENT INFLUENCE

There are college presidents and trustees who say the only way to surmount the critical financial problems facing the private colleges and universities of the nation is by turning to Washington for more federal aid. Other educational leaders feel that "he who pays the piper calls the tune", and if the Federal government provides massive subsidies it will exert a controlling influence on our higher institutions. Such government influence or control might, in the estimation of Wickham[8] and other thoughtful presidents, constitute a serious threat to our dual system of public and private higher education.

Some educational leaders claim that the independent institutions may be freer from political influence than the tax-supported institutions, but that this is a relative situation varying in each institution. Trustees of publicly supported institutions say that the great municipal colleges and outstanding state universities are not being subverted or dictated to by their Boards of Estimate or legislatures. Then, too, the independent institutions are now receiving considerable support from the Federal government for buildings and scholarships, and from both the government and the giant corporations for contractual scientific research, but there has been no attempt on the part of either to influence the recipient institutions.

However, it is possible that should inadequate financing cause the private institutions to disappear, a single system of higher education might develop to the point where government control could follow government support. One way to combat any such situation is to keep the private colleges strong. Research conducted at several European institutions indicates that another way to preserve independence, assuming the private colleges were given considerable government support, would be to adopt a policy similar to that used by Britain in distributing funds from the Exchequer to the universities through a University Grants Committee.[9] The University Grants Committee was established by Parliament to serve as a liaison group between the government and the universities. It is composed of men broadly representative (in terms of geographical, occupational, economic, social and political backgrounds) of the British people. If any one group on the committee has a greater numerical representation than the others, it is the professional educators.

PERSONNEL SHORTAGES

Personnel shortages have long been a problem to American colleges and universities. Until recently, the greatest shortage was found in several of the scholarly disciplines such as the humanities and the sciences. Some shortages still exist for qualified faculty members because of an insufficient number being graduated in certain subject fields and because industry attracts away the key men by offering higher salaries, especially in the sciences. However, enlightened boards have encouraged their graduate and professional schools to turn out more people in the critical areas and trustees have insisted that faculty salaries (especially in the larger universities) must compare favorably to industrial salaries.

Personnel shortages also exist in the administrative or

executive side of higher education. Not only are there insufficient administrators available, but some of the people
holding executive positions in colleges and universities are
clearly incompetent. A genuine effort is needed on the part
of leaders in the corporations (as financial backers), in the
foundations (as locators of talent), and in the universities
(as training centers) to eliminate this condition. Trustees
have a responsibility for calling forth that genuine effort.

It is unfortunate that college boards, because of shortages of qualified personnel, frequently hire as college and
university presidents persons who are unqualified in experience and unsuited in temperament to the demands of
the presidency. It is ironical that these trustees frequently reach into the military establishments for commanders
and into the classroom for professors, some of whom have
had no experience in academic administration. These presidential candidates take on this specialized task reluctantly,
struggle with it unsuccessfully for an average of eight years,
and leave it as bitter and frustrated individuals.[10]

In addition to the necessity for careful selection of presidents, the trustees themselves must be chosen carefully
and oriented properly to their heavy responsibility, a major
part of which is the selection of the chief executive officer.
When they exercise this function and elect a president, it
should be a man qualified for the job by education, experience and personality.

On the latter subject—providing specialized education
and professional experience for future presidents and other
administrators—the major universities have a serious responsibility. Only in the past few years has there been a
genuine and fairly widespread acceptance of the notion
that college administration is as much a science as an art—

that administrators are *made* as well as *born*. (This point is documented and expanded in greater detail in later chapters.)[11]

Higher education has such an essential role in the educational scheme at this stage of civilization that the colleges and universities need better educational leadership and administrative direction than they have had. We are still in a period of changing conceptions as to the nature and scope of higher education, and hence there is unusual demand for creative imagination and courage in the building of group morale and the attaining of public confidence in the changes that are made.

ENROLLMENT PROBLEMS

Enrollment problems constitute the fourth major threat. Many colleges and universities are hard-pressed properly to educate the enormous numbers of young people who are now enrolling. This is especially true in the tax-supported institutions that are required to accept all high school graduates in their state. This problem can be solved if existing institutions are expanded, new institutions built and several venerable academic traditions and customs carefully re-examined. The first and second solutions are obvious—the third needs further explanation.

Since the first colleges and universities opened in this nation, it has been customary for most classes to meet in the morning, for laboratory periods and a few classes to occur in the afternoon, and seldom are formal meetings of undergraduate academic groups held in the evenings. In addition, Saturdays and Sundays have been set aside as days of worship and contemplation, rest and relaxation. Long vacations, especially in the summer, compound this problem. In consequence of this, there is on many of our campuses considerable wasted space in buildings. Sooner or later such inefficient management of space and schedules must be corrected. Student and faculty resistance to afternoon, evening and weekend classes, laboratories and seminars must be overcome. Legislatures will not appropriate, nor donors contribute, the amounts of money necessary to cope with the expected peaks of enrollment and general phenomenal growth under existing conditions. Certainly they will not provide funds for more new buildings if those available are not properly used.

It should be possible by proper allocation of physical facilities to essential academic programs to accommodate a sizeable portion of the increased numbers expected. If careful scheduling is coupled with reasonable expansion of existing plants and some construction of new buildings, this difficult problem of crowding can be eased. The increasing development of two-year junior colleges will also help to solve this problem. With many more children actually in the high schools and a greater percentage of them wanting to go to college, no effort should be spared to accommodate these future leaders of America.

MEETING THE CHALLENGES

There are serious problems that threaten higher education and there are magnificent opportunities that challenge it. Given the appropriate understanding by the public, adequate lay leadership by trustees, insightful professional leadership by administrators, and inspired teaching by faculty members, higher education today—and tomorrow—will rise to new heights of service to the nation and to humanity.

DOCUMENTATION AND COMMENTARY

[1] Gerald P. Burns, *Report of a Study of Finance and Administration in Asia,* New York: The Sloan Foundation, 1962, p. 37.

[2] Clarence A. Schoenfeld, *The University and Its Publics,* New York: Harper & Row, 1954, p. 3.

[3] Henry M. Wriston, "Principles Governing Requests for Educational Institutions," *School & Society,* 77: March 28, 1953, p. 193.

[4] Beardsley Ruml and Donald H. Morrison, *Memo to a College Trustee,* New York: McGraw-Hill Book Company, 1959, p. 13.

[5] Algo D. Henderson, *Policies and Practices in Higher Education,* New York: Harper & Row, 1960, p. 232.

[6] For further information of value on extra-curricular and co-curricular programs, see Nevitt Sanford, *The American College,* New York: John Wiley & Sons, 1962.

[7] U. S. Office of Education, *Biennial Survey of Education in the United States,* March 1960, Chapter 4, Section II.

[8] W. T. Wickham, "Annual Report to the Board of Trustees, Independent College Funds of America, Inc.", New York: January 1960.

[9] Gerald P. Burns, *Summary of Survey of University Finance in Europe,* New York: The Ford Foundation, 1960, p. 4.

[10] Harold Taylor, as reported in the *New York Times,* November 22, 1959.

[11] Proceedings of the Sloan Foundation Conferences on the Shortage of University Administrators, New York: January 1962.

THEORY AND PRACTICE
3 IN ACADEMIC
GOVERNANCE

The growth of the trusteeship into its present importance
and relationship with the administration has been gradual
and has been slowly changing with the times. In weighing
the need for external lay leadership, it is clear that a greatly
strengthened presidency could have met this need, as indeed it was met by exceptional men at various times in various institutions.[1] In retrospect, however, it appears that the
president's responsibilities expanded too rapidly to be man-
ageable concurrently with the disappearance of a coherent
curriculum and a unified faculty. Thus trustees arrived on
the scene and began to play an ever-increasing role in
governing American colleges and universities.

THEORETICAL CONSIDERATIONS

At the start of the 20th century, Cattell indicated that the
role of the trustees and the administration in colleges and

universities was actually so strong as to be "utterly subversive of a true democracy."[2] He felt that a huge bureaucracy had been established that was not working in the best interests of the higher institutions, and that the techniques of big business had been "wantonly" applied to university administration and governance in this country. Cattell further said (in 1906) that we are between the "Scylla of presidential autocracy and the Charybdis of faculty and trustee incompetence", and that the university must be completely reorganized. It was his thesis that American higher institutions should return governance and administration to the faculty, students and alumni.

In contrasting these notions with what current leaders in the field believe, the conclusion is drawn that Cattell had either a different perspective or a distorted impression of the function of administration and governance. Nature abhors a vacuum; and since at least a partial vacuum existed in terms of a lack of adequate faculty and alumni leadership in governance in the colonial colleges, it is natural that lay leadership took over. As the frontier was pushed back and as American colleges matured differently from their European progenitors, this kind of lay or external governance became a permanent and logical adjunct in higher education.

In the current situation, the trusteeship appears to be more of an art than a science. The general philosophy of this lay approach to governance was clearly stated by Tead. He said the primary responsibilities of the trustees are: "(1) to understand the human and national purpose which the university or college is designed to serve, (2) to gain a genuine intimacy with at least some phases of operation in the specific institution, and (3) to approach the entire effort with a deep sense of affection for the value of higher education in general and for one's own college in particular."[3] This plea for understanding of, intimacy with, and affection for one's institution first and all higher education second, is reasonable for all trustees who seek success for their efforts, and satisfaction for their desires in aiding and assisting as board members.

INTERNAL RELATIONSHIPS

There are two general areas of the trustee's relationships (internal and external) that deserve mention in describing the existing pattern. The internal relationships are between trustees and their chairman, president, administrators, faculty and students.

The trustees, quite properly, look to their chairman for leadership, inspiration and stimuluation. It is generally accepted that the chairman is the pivotal person and should have the genuine support of all board members.

As the key man in operational matters, the college president occupies the position as the executive officer under the chairman. Trustees act with him officially as a group on policy matters and unofficially as individuals for purposes of advice and assistance.

With the other administrators, trustees also have to play two different roles. Acting always as a group, their decisions are handed to the administrators through the president. Unofficially and individually, however, they can be very helpful in providing direct assistance in their areas of special competence (e.g., legal, medical, financial, etc.).

There is general agreement in the field that individual board members should not act unilaterally with faculty members or students. Their relationship with the faculty should be warm and friendly, sensitive and sympathetic, helpful and considerate. Lobbying by faculty should be discouraged. Further agreement exists that trustees should make special efforts to understand the problems and potentialities of the student body. This can be rewarding both personally and professionally.

EXTERNAL RELATIONSHIPS

The concept of identifiable groups among which relationships develop includes a university "family of five members: the board of trustees or regents, the administration, the faculty, the students, and the public."[4] Actually, there are at least three special external groups, in addition to the "general public", with whom trustees have particular relationships . . . alumni, supporters, and friends of the institution.

Trustees are frequently selected from the alumni of the institution. For that reason, the board can and should maintain close rapport with former students of the college or university. This is a vitally important "public" to the institution.

Every institution needs financial support from off-campus, whether it is the legislature (for the public colleges) or voluntary donors (for the private colleges). The trustees have a special obligation to encourage sources of financial aid. With legislators this encouragement usually takes the shape of maintaining their confidence and active interest in the institution. With donors from the private sectors, this encouragement usually takes the shape of securing their good will and approbation of the institution.

Lastly, the institution seeks *friends* from within the citizenry or the general public in the institution's operating area (be it international, national, regional, statewide, or metropolitan) because ultimately, support (either moral or financial) comes from friends. Reports from the member institutions of the Independent College Funds of America, Inc., indicate that this support flows most freely from a friendly, confident, informed people. In many ways they look to the trustees for interpretation of the institution and as representatives of the institution upon which to base their confidence, friendship and finally, financial support.

THE TRUSTEE'S ROLE DEFINED BRIEFLY

The role of the trustees as members of a board is legislative, not executive. As members of a board or council, they should work together in democratic fashion with decisions arrived at by majority vote. Their influence, then, is collective and they act as a body. A brief description of the function of these individuals might be found in the words Wriston frequently used, saying their role involved "work, wealth and wisdom." They are expected to give considerable time, material support and sound judgment to their responsibilities.

THE GENERAL INFLUENCE

The board of trustees is the legal entity of the institution. The board has the responsibility and authority to govern the college or university in accordance with the charter or articles of incorporation approved for it by the state in which it is located. In some ways the influence of the board goes beyond its strictly legal scope, and in some ways it never reaches (or at least exercises) its full legal responsibility. Many experienced trustees feel that fundamental as such legal prescriptions are, still more important is the spirit by which the letter of the law is interpreted and applied. This spirit is to be found in the actual procedure of the board and the personality of its membership. Although it defies description, this elusive thing called "spirit" is intimately related to the influence of the board in any given situation.

THE GENERAL EFFECT

The general effect of this relaxed holding of authority and responsibility has seemed to be salutary in most cases. It has given rise to a delegation, quite properly, of authority for the management of the institution to the president. The trustees have retained, in most instances, general control of finances and the faculty has secured control of the educational program. On this latter point, Carmichael says, "The most serious gap in the organization of higher education in the English speaking world is the lack of provision for realistic and systematic attention to broad educational programs, policies and practices."[5]

It is clearly the responsibility of the president and trustees to mobilize and manage the physical and financial resources necessary to support the academic program which the faculty has determined. This pattern of shared responsibility for various facets of the institution's operations has been in popular usage for the past century.

The influence of the board flows from the legal power with which it is vested. It also derives influence from the social, economic, and political status of its individual members. The immediate effect of its influence is seldom as great as if it exercised that authority which it possesses. As a rule, trustees are conservative in their views and actions. Frequently, it is the executive committee of the board that moves the majority into new departures and provides a liberal or progressive approach to problems.

The trustees have no simple task in guiding the destinies of their institutions. These institutions are constantly challenged by the necessity for adapting their curriculum to keep pace with society's needs, and they are handicapped by what appears to be the widest dispersal of decision-making authority found in any social institution. Thus the college or university is frequently threatened by the consequences of such lack of direction. Since universities have survived for eight centuries, have grown and are growing, and have exercised influence over the society that obtains wherever they are, it appears that these institutions have possessed the leadership that was required. The task of leadership in higher education is that of utilizing human, financial, physical and spiritual resources to fashion a college or university that welcomes new methods and programs but maintains the enduring values.

The leadership responsibilities of the trustees may be examined best by an analysis of the major functions which the board influences. These functions cover a wide range of activities, from selecting fellow trustees to approving the annual budget. The sections below examine the validity of the hypothesis that the role played by the trustee exerts a profound influence on the institution.

THE STRENGTHS AND WEAKNESSES OF THE BOARD

The standards or criteria for determining the strength or power, and the weakness or apathy of any board are relative and arbitrary. The determination of what constitutes a strong or a weak role should rest upon the degree of leadership or decision-making carried on by the board. For example, it is clear that the trustees play a strong role in establishing financial policy; it is equally clear that they play a weak role in the development of curriculum.

The strength or weakness of the trustee's role in the administrative area is obvious, primarily because of the board's relationship to the president. The role is a strong and highly important one in this area. Although most of their operations flow through the president, there is frequently close contact between trustees and other top administrators.

Lloyd has pointed out, "Whatever the responsibilities of trustees have been in the past, there is no longer a shadow of a doubt that they will be quite specific and substantial in the years ahead. The functions of trustees can not be sharply divided in any categorical manner from those of administrative officers and faculties. Their functions are integrated into the operations of a university at all levels, but where purposes and objectives are clearly defined and if good will and restraints are strong enough, there will be almost no conflict among these three groups. This is the way it should be."[6] There is little doubt but that the trustees will continue to function in close proximity to the administration.

One of the desirable reasons for faculty and administrators cooperating more closely with trustees is the fact that many faculty members have looked down on management functions. It is unfortunately true that the downgrading of university administration in the hierarchy of academic values is a real barrier to improvement. Distinguished academicians have admitted that since efficiency can be achieved only by widespread faculty participation, lay and administrative leadership must be supported. More intimate professional association and enlarged non-professional contact should help to provide mutual understanding and greater cooperation.

The Manual for Trustees published by Columbia University indicated, ". . . that the administration of university affairs is quite a different matter from the pursuit of learning is indeed a statement to which this Committee assents, believing also that high aptitudes for both are seldom found in the same person."[7] I disagree with this view. What is needed in the presidency is "a man of management" and "a man of learning." The same man *can* incorporate both qualities.[8]

Many leaders in business, industry, finance, and the foundations are asking trustees why college administration or university management is so often downgraded by the teaching faculties. Perhaps one answer to this is that college administration falls into a limbo between business administration and college teaching. In recent years there have been some trends that indicate a reversal of this downgrading. In weighing these trends, one observes that there is ample room in higher education for the professional administrator.[9] This career provides profound satisfaction, both personal and professional. However, along with that is usually found some frustration, many disappointments, and occasional heartbreak.

Because of their close relationship with the administration, the trustees are in a strategic position to see that personnel policy in this matter of securing qualified educational executives for their institution is well developed, carefully tested, and correctly implemented. Selecting, hiring and training the staff is the responsibility of the president, but the trustees may advise and assist in this matter.

PRACTICAL CONSIDERATIONS

With respect to the board's promotion of administrators, a general principle recognized by good management is that of promoting from within whenever possible. However, the board should not be bound by this dictum, since people, circumstances and institutions vary greatly. Other factors being equal, where it is possible to find qualified men within the faculty or staff, they should be considered for administrative positions.

In electing the president, experience has proven that to take a man from the classroom or laboratory and thrust him directly into the presidency usually is unfair to both the man and the institution. Weight of opinion appears on the side of securing a president, or other top administrator, from one's own or some other educational institution; securing a man who has taught and who is a scholar, *but* who has also had some previous administrative experience. With respect to promoting from within, Burgess says the first duty of the board in thinking about succession, ". . . is to select the president of the university and also . . . to have a hand in selecting the officer or officers who in the normal course of promotion may succeed . . . to the presidency."[10] This practice is common in business and industry; it helps to keep morale high and provide for continuity of succession.

Boards of trustees must have close rapport and a strong role with, or relationship to, their college's administration. However, the majority of the board members, mindful of their *legislative* (rather than *executive*) function, scrupulously avoid interfering in the operations of the institution.

It appears that some boards tend toward conservatism, if not timidity, in their reluctance to "start" anything, even in these days when many starts are indicated. There is an archaic code of courtesy which does not always operate for the institution's welfare.[11]

There are some writers who think of governance and administration as the same function . . . a function that is not too well performed. For example, Paton has observed that the development of our American universities is handicapped by the current system of administration and that "trustees see things through a glass, very darkly."[12] Not many students of the field agree with this view. Indeed, as indicated earlier in this section and below, it appears that most writers concur that the trustee's role with respect to administration is clear and that it will exert considerable effect on the future of higher education in America. Indeed, there is general acceptance of Lloyd's theory, that the trustee is a vital factor in the university and the university is a vital factor in our civilization. "Private colleges and universities simply must not fail to carry the torch for the highest possible standards of scholarship and research. They must not fail to continue as the bulwarks of independent thought and action and as centers of impartiality and integrity in the criticism of public affairs. For, would they fail in these respects, then this whole delicate structure of our national life—and its leadership in the free world, and, possibly, in the entire world—may suffer and gradually deteriorate."[13]

From the foregoing discussion it appears that there are various strengths and weaknesses attributed to the role of the board members with respect to certain facets of our colleges and universities. Trustees play a small role in curricular matters, but it may be gaining strength; they play an unimportant role with students, and this seems to be constant; they play a more important role in faculty matters, and this should be expanded; they play their most important role with the administration and this too, is constant.

DOCUMENTATION AND COMMENTARY

[1] Beardsley Ruml and Donald H. Morrison, *Memo to a College Trustee,* New York: McGraw-Hill Company, 1959, p. 50.

[2] J. McKeen Cattell, *University Control,* New York: The Science Press, 1913, p. 14.

[3] Ordway Tead, *Trustees, Teachers and Students,* Salt Lake City: University of Utah Press, 1951, p. 1.

[4] Arthur S. Adams, "The University Family," *Proceedings,* Utah Conference on Higher Education, 1951, p. 51.

[5] Oliver C. Carmichael, *Universities: Commonwealth and American,* New York: Harper and Brothers, 1959, p. 105.

[6] Glen Lloyd, "Blueprint for Trustees", *The University of Chicago Magazine,* Spring, 1960, p. 11.

[7] William S. Paley, "The Role of the Trustees of Columbia University", New York: Columbia University, November 4, 1957.

[8] Harold W. Stoke, *The American College President,* New York: Harper and Row, 1958, p. 39.

[9] Henry M. Wriston, "Looking at the College Presidency in Retrospect", Association of American Colleges *Bulletin,* December 1955, p. 41.

[10] Kenneth F. Burgess, "The Trustee's Function in Today's Universities and Colleges," Association of American Colleges *Bulletin,* October 1958, p. 44.

[11] Robert Duncan, *College Trustees, Fund-Raising and Public Relations,* Washington: American Alumni Council, 1960, p. 11.

[12] Stewart Paton, "University Administration and University Ideals," *Science,* November 1911, p. 34.

[13] Lloyd, *op. cit.,* p. 10.

4 ADMINISTRATION OF HIGHER EDUCATION

While some overlap continues to exist and may be considered tolerable between *governance,* as the function of the board, and *administration,* as the function of the staff, the two operations are quite different. Trustees, in governing the institution, act in a kind of legislative capacity. Theirs is primarily a group-oriented leadership that paints in broad strokes the policy picture of the college or university. The president and his staff, in administering the institution, act in a kind of managerial capacity. They function chiefly as executives responsible for general operations (in the case of the president) or specific operations (in the case of other administrators).

THE ROLE OF ADMINISTRATION

Administration is a leadership and a managerial function. The over-riding responsibility of all administrators, including the president, is to operate the institution and its varying facets in the most effective, efficient and economical fashion. A single, unifying viewpoint should prevail in the administrative structure of every institution: it is that administration exists for the purpose of facilitating, enabling and operating the total program of the college or university. Administration must be academically oriented, for it is recognized that the great aims and objectives of higher education can be achieved best when all the plant, personnel, and financial operations are effectively coordinated to serve the academic program.

ORGANIZATION OF COLLEGES AND UNIVERSITIES

In general, colleges and universities operate under policies established by the board and interpreted by the president. In consequence of that, the president is the chief executive and administrative officer. Depending upon the size and complexity of the institution, he is aided by various vice presidents, deans, directors and assistants. Functions of these administrators are briefly described in subsequent sections of this chapter. In the main, these functions are similar, but not identical, in all higher institutions. The hierarchy of the administrative structure in the typical small college and large university are indicated herein. These should be considered as approximate or recommended groupings for the following reasons: First, no two institutions are exactly alike; secondly, function must determine structure; thirdly, job assignments vary with individual qualifications; fourthly, education is dynamic and change is the only constant.

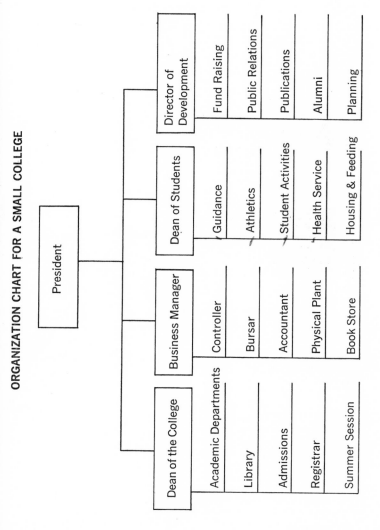

ORGANIZATION CHART FOR A SMALL COLLEGE

President

Dean of the College
- Academic Departments
- Library
- Admissions
- Registrar
- Summer Session

Business Manager
- Controller
- Bursar
- Accountant
- Physical Plant
- Book Store

Dean of Students
- Guidance
- Athletics
- Student Activities
- Health Service
- Housing & Feeding

Director of Development
- Fund Raising
- Public Relations
- Publications
- Alumni
- Planning

ORGANIZATION CHART FOR A LARGE UNIVERSITY

President

Executive Vice President Academic Affairs	Senior Vice President Developmental Affairs	Vice Pres.-Treas. Business Affairs	Vice President Student Affairs	Vice President University Affairs
Undergraduate College Deans	Director of Inst. Research & Planning	Bursar and Controller	Deans of Men and Women	Director of Libraries
Graduate & Professional School Deans	Director of Development	Director of Auditing and Accounting	Director of Health Service	Director of Admissions
Director of Summer Session	Director of Public Relations	Director of Personnel	Director of Athletics	Director of Registration
Director of Exchange Programs	Director of Publications	Director of Buildings and Grounds	Director of Guidance and Counseling	Director of Auxiliary Enterprises
Director of Extension Programs	Director of Alumni Programs	Director of Purchasing	Director of Placement and Student Aid	Director of University Press

OFFICE OF THE PRESIDENT

The main function of the president is to preside over the institution and to lead it toward the fulfillment of its objectives. While serving as its chief executive officer under the board of trustees, he must be the inspiration and embodiment of the entire enterprise, giving life and spirit to the "shadow" of the institution.

Collegiate institutions are so diverse and their characters change with such frequency that it is difficult, if not impossible, to describe the average or typical president. However, there are many traits, requirements and responsibilities that presidents generally hold in common.

While the title is usually the same for the chief executive in business as in education, his basic philosophy of operation is quite different. For example, the only "profit" a college president must show is continued excellence in students graduating. He should balance the budget, but, it is more important that a high quality of intellectual activity be offered. He is at once the boss and servant of his faculty; although technically he is employed by the board, faculties have been known to force out college presidents.

The essential operations of the president are concerned with people. He works for the board, through his administrators, with the faculty, to educate the students. These four groups constitute his interacting publics. There are other identifiable individuals and groups with which he must deal to a lesser extent (*i.e.*, alumni, parents, donors, legislators, accrediting bodies, supervisory bodies, professional associations, and friends of the institution).

The president is in frequent contact with the important people in each group. In the case of the trustees, it's the board and committee chairmen; with the administration, it's the vice presidents and deans; with the faculty, it's the department heads and senior professors; with the students, it's the president of the student body and leaders of the student organizations.

The wise president will exert persuasive influence on all these groups, but will not attempt to master all operational details, render total leadership, or attend every meeting. He will decentralize operations and delegate responsibility to the fullest extent compatible with his own schedule, the qualifications of the persons concerned, and the complexity of the responsibilities involved.

A sizeable portion of the president's time will be devoted to correspondence. He must maintain clear and frequent communication with his key people in each group. The board, the other administrators, the faculty, the student body (and to a lesser extent, all related groups) must be kept informed.

The experience of great presidents and outstanding institutions has proven conclusively that one of the serious handicaps faced by the American college or university president is overwork. When such occurs, the institution and all its constituents suffer. There is no one way to avoid presidential overload, because all presidents and institutional problems differ. But, if properly selected for endurance and ability, if adequately supported by the board and if skillfully assisted by his staff, a president will be shielded from this problem.

Benezet has pointed out that a president must think, act, and care.[1] He must *think* clearly about all major issues facing his institution. He must *act* decisively, for action is the crux of his office. He must *care* deeply because he is ultimately responsible for the entire institution.

The president has a responsibility to the board that is sometimes misunderstood or overlooked. As the senior professional educator of the enterprise, one of his main tasks is presenting to the lay board suggestions for policy. Further, he must have alternatives, reasons for his suggestions, and the ability to move the board toward a consensus. If he is a skillful and resourceful leader, he will elicit from his trustees not only sound statements of policy, but advice on and invaluable assistance in effectively implementing the new or reformulated policy. As indicated in other sections of this study, he is also responsible for "educating" the board and providing the orientation needed.

ACADEMIC MANAGEMENT

As indicated in the organization charts of all higher institutions, the most important operation on campus is the academic. Originally this area included all aspects of the curriculum (classes, laboratories, seminars), co-curriculum (special lectures, related research, collateral reading) and extra-curricular activities (sports, socials, student affairs).

As colleges and universities grew in size and expanded in offerings, a division occurred which split the purely academic affairs (curriculum) and the less fomal co- and extra-curricular programs. This section will deal with the former; a subsequent section will deal with the latter.

Leadership of the academic program is usually delegated by the president to the vice president for academic affairs, the dean of faculty, or the dean of the college. The person occupying this post, regardless of title, is usually the second-ranking administrative officer on campus. Sometimes he holds the title of executive or senior vice president; occasionally he is called provost or chancellor. In a typical university, the deans of the various undergraduate, graduate and professional colleges report to the academic vice president. At the college level the academic department chairmen report to the dean. These academic officers (deans) invariably come up through the faculty ranks and sometimes maintain their professorial status by continuing to teach one or two courses.

The basic purpose of the college or university is to provide quality education for its students. The basic purpose of academic management within the institution is to provide the actual curriculum or courses of study in which this education takes place.

In addition to the vice presidents and deans, the academic areas have other administrative officers (as indicated on the organization charts). Chief among these others are the directors of the library, admissions and registration. Other functions sometimes operated within this area are summer session, extension, and exchange programs. Occasionally, some of these operations are listed under the student affairs area, or under university affairs.

The faculty comprises the largest professional group in the institution. Members of the faculty usually teach in academic departments or divisions related to the scholarly disciplines. As a rule, departments or divisions are headed up by chairmen elected by the faculty or appointed by the administration. The faculty is usually represented by an elected council or senate which crosses departmental lines.

Much has been written about faculty leadership. If one might attempt to summarize some of the research and practice in this facet of higher education, it could be done by offering two brief and general suggestions for academic management: Since faculty members are essentially individualists dedicated to a scholarly discipline, they should be handled accordingly. For best results, academic administration (whether at the level of president, vice president, dean or department head) should be conducted in a low key by engineered consent and agreement, rather than by enforced command and fiat.[2]

BUSINESS MANAGEMENT

Another major administrative area in higher institutions is that concerned with the business management of the enterprise. Most presidents are better prepared to direct the academic affairs than to direct the business affairs of their schools. Consequently, every collegiate institution has a senior officer under the president charged with the responsibility for administering and coordinating all the business and financial operations.

There are five or six basic divisions or departments within this area. In small institutions, they are sometimes combined; in large institutions, they are sometimes sub-divided; but, as functions, they exist in every institution. They are the operation of the physical plant, accounting, personnel services, purchasing, housing and feeding. In addition to these six, there are several auxiliary or miscellaneous functions (*i.e.*, bookstore operation) that may or may not come under the supervision of the chief business officer.

Although the president is ultimately responsible for the budget, the chief academic officer and the chief business officer frequently help to formulate it. For this reason a budget officer is sometimes found in the business and financial area. Since the budget is the principal instrument for administering the education departments and their programs, the chief business officer must be educationally oriented.

In many institutions, the business manager is also the treasurer. Reduced to its simplest meaning, this extra title implies a responsibility for the receipt, disbursement, and custody of funds. In colleges and universities with large endowments, the treasurer may assume operational responsibility for the investment portfolio. In a few institutions, a member of the board will be found serving as treasurer.

The role of the business officer as watchdog of the assets and expenditures of the institution is important and difficult. Financial limitations frequently require that he restrain the faculty, other administrators, and even the president, when their enthusiasm for new and costly education programs would lead to financial problems. But this is a primary function of business management and it calls for an able and tactful administrator.

STUDENT LEADERSHIP

A third major area in college and university administration is that of student services. The functions provided under this title should be considered essential, but auxiliary, to the instructional effort. There are three major areas: *student welfare services,* with the health service, testing and counseling, placement service and financial aid (loans, scholarships, etc.); *student activities services,* with co- and extra-curricular programs such as student government, student organizations, social, cultural and athletic activities; *student control services,* with such functions as discipline, guidance, living group supervision and religion. As indicated on the earlier organization charts, some of these functions are interchangeable with other major areas of operation.[3]

Historically, student personnel administration in American institutions, like so many of our educational traditions, traces back to the British universities where the college as a living group was responsible for the housing, feeding, and protection of students, as well as for providing educational programs.[4] This centralized and coordinated non-academic program for students is mainly justified from a management viewpoint by its efficient contribution to student life and, thus, enabling the institution to carry out its basic educational purpose most effectively.

In the larger university, this area is directed by a vice president for student affairs. In the smaller college, this area is directed by a dean of students. The head of this area, and his principal subordinates, must be sound educators, must have a grounding in psychology, must have pleasing personalities, and must have patient temperaments.

By guiding with a light touch the extra-curricular life of the college or university, the vice president or dean of students is facilitating institutional purposes by providing a controllable laboratory of human relations for immediate testing of academic principles. Desirable contacts, interactions, and relationships arranged by design or occurring by chance between and among faculty and students create learning situations of great value. Education need not be limited to the classrooms and laboratories; capable leaders in student affairs will see to it that optimum conditions prevail on their campus for maximizing informal cultural and educational possibilities.

PROMOTIONAL LEADERSHIP

The fourth major area of administration is that dealing with the development and advancement of the institution.

Trustees are usually more familiar with the functions of this division than those three preceding it.

The functions usually grouped in this area are fund-raising, public relations, alumni affairs, and institutional planning. In addition, one frequently finds in the larger institutions, offices of public information, publications, radio and television, government relations and university press in this division. Because this is the newest and most fluid area of the institution's operations, these functions occupy no set position or pattern and are frequently added to (or deleted from) the area.

Since no college or university admits to having enough money to do the job it has set for itself, every institution is concerned with improving its image, gaining greater understanding, winning new friends and expanding its gift income. For this reason, nearly every institution, even those being tax-supported, now has at least one person assigned to "development".

In the larger schools, this person is called vice president for development, or something similar; in the smaller schools, this person is called director of development or assistant to the president. Regardless of his title, his function is to promote the interests of the institution along all possible avenues and his main job is to achieve an ever rising level of financial support.[5] His secondary responsibilities relate to this in various ways from the more direct (*i.e.*, improved public relations and expanding alumni fund) to the rather indirect (*i.e.*, effective student recruiting, publications and successful university press operations).

Usually the head of this area serves on the level with the other vice presidents (or deans and directors). However, the financial situation has become so critical in many of the private institutions, that this post is considered second in importance only to the president.[6] In some of the larger private universities where there are several vice presidents, he is (like the academic head) given the additional title of *executive* or *senior* vice president. Indeed, although this practice is generally frowned upon, in order to secure the services of top flight development officers, several institutions have raised the remuneration for this assignment above that of the president.

As indicated earlier, the promotional or developmental area is sometimes looked down upon by the academicians. This is understandable since most teachers do not fully comprehend the need for (or purpose of) the functions carried out. Until recently, practitioners in public relations and development were considered apart from other educators because they had few academic qualifications or interests. However, as this area continues to expand in size and importance, a new breed of professionals is surging to the front. Many of these new men came out of faculty ranks and hold the Ph.D.; many have had special administrative training and external experience in promotional affairs. Some of these have gone beyond their associates and been elected presidents of leading institutions throughout the nation.

Among the chief tasks in this area is the proper interpretation of the institution. Skill in communication of various kinds is essential in this function. Closely related to this is fund-raising of all types, including the alumni fund campaigns. Collateral activities include cultivating and soliciting trustees, wealthy individuals, parents and, sometimes, students. Certainly corporations and foundations must not be overlooked. All of these sensitive and difficult operations must be carefully planned, scheduled and coordinated by the vice president or director of development—if not the president himself.

In the early days funds were raised for colleges in response to an immediate need. If the roof leaked, money was raised to repair it; if a student needed financial assistance, a patron was found to help; if a building was needed, a fund drive was launched. The majority of institutions today eschew this pattern and make long-range plans to insure future financial stability. Today, development is viewed as a continuous process with specific goals, phase lines, gift tables, and target dates by which particular parts of the over-all "blueprint" are to be accomplished. The old fashioned fund drive is transformed into a scientific campaign and integrated into the long-range operational plan. Such careful planning enables various individuals and groups to participate in the program at different times, and it ensures that operating income and capital funds will be received on a scheduled basis.

SUMMARY OF ADMINISTRATION

Just as administration is essential in the industrial company (to lead and coordinate production, sales, distribution, advertising, finance, and purchasing), so too, it is essential in higher education. The educational potential of any institution is frequently determined by its organization and administration.[7] Some centralization is undoubtedly needed for an effective program of education, but too much centralization can easily result in rigid and undesirable control. The best administered institutions in America exhibit good balance between centralization and decentralization. The best administered institutions in Europe display a distinct tendency toward decentralization. The best administered institutions in Asia indicate a conspicuous leaning toward centralization. There are desirable elements in each and there is no pat formula that applies to every college or university.[8]

Riesman and Jencks claim that the "teaching is amateurish" and the over-all operation of higher institutions is "frequently chaotic and improvised" without being creative. They go on to say that with the exception of the Harvard Business School giving some minimum training to college administrators, little help is offered. They conclude by saying that this paucity of training opportunities is caused by the envy and resentment that college faculty members have against "bureaucrats".[9] While the evidence against these statements is monumental, since dozens of higher institutions now offer courses in college administration, the comments serve to emphasize that there is room for improvement. Certainly more and better training for administrators should be offered.[10] In addition, perhaps some enterprising institution will follow the Reed College-University of Oregon's "Trustee Conference" by offering a course or seminar for trustees on *administration* or for administrators on the *trusteeship*.

DOCUMENTATION AND COMMENTARY

[1] Louis T. Benezet, "The Office of the President", Gerald P. Burns (Ed.) *Administrators in Higher Education,* New York: Harper and Row, 1962, p. 108.

[2] Harold W. Dodds, *The Academic President-Educator or Caretaker,* New York: McGraw-Hill Company, 1962, p. 132.

[3] This interchange is especially noticeable in the housing and food serving functions which are sometimes placed under the business affairs office and sometimes under the student affairs office.

[4] Charles W. Bursch, "The Vice President or Dean of Students", Gerald P. Burns, (Ed.) *Administrators in Higher Education,* New York: Harper and Row, 1962, p. 144.

[5] John A. Pollard, *Fund Raising for Higher Education,* New York: Harper and Row, 1958, p. 88.

[6] Harold Dodds in *The Academic President—Educator or Caretaker* makes a strong case for each president having an alter ego. Since many presidents are temperamentally opposed to promotional activities, many development officers have earned the confidence of their chiefs and are serving in the role of junior partner or assistant president.

[7] Theodore L. Reller, and Edgar L. Morphet, (Ed.) *Comparative Educational Administration,* Englewood Cliffs, New Jersey: Prentice-Hall, Inc., 1962, p. 398.

[8] Gerald P. Burns, "Financing Universities in Europe", *School and Society,* March 11, 1961, Vol. 89, No. 2188.

[9] Nevitt Sanford, *The American College,* New York: John Wiley and Sons, 1962, p. 101.

[10] Although this writer and presidents of other large national organizations in the field of higher education have long urged acceptance of the notion that college administration should be considered a bona fide professional discipline, it was not until the 1964 annual conference of the Association for Higher Education that this was adopted. The conference endorsed the obvious fact that a "managerial revolution" was occurring in higher education and that colleges and universities should become aware of it. The points were made that the philanthropic foundations and the great universities should cooperate in expanding enormously opportunities for graduate study and internship experience in administration in order to produce qualified educational executives for the higher institutions.

5 SELECTION AND ORIENTATION OF TRUSTEES

The qualifications upon which trustees are selected are many and varied. The selection process itself differs in higher institutions. Once qualifications are determined and selection made, then the new trustee must be given information on his institution and an introduction to his role on the board.

SELECTION OF TRUSTEES

College and university trustees are chosen or recruited in many ways. In the private institutions, the president usually keeps a list of prominent persons that he would like someday to have as board members. As a rule, they are persons who have some connection with or interest in the college or university. When there is a vacancy on the board, the president presents one or more names to the chairman

63

who, in turn, passes them along to the nominating committee. This committee then screens the candidates, discusses
them with the board chairman and the president, and those
who pass muster are asked "if elected, would you serve?"

The president is not the sole instigator of the action. Frequently, his development officer, alumni director or other
staff members will come up with worthy candidates. And,
not infrequently, the chairman or other board members
will have suggestions. Indeed, occasionally persons outside
the institutional orbit—persons in foundations, corporations, government and even other institutions—will offer
recommendations.

In the case of public colleges and universities, while the
institutional staff and its board can suggest candidates,
since the board seldom elects, the suggestions are passed
along to the appointing authority. Generally the appointing authority—the Mayor, Governor, or President—because of political implications, has a list of his own that re-
ceives priority. Occasionally the legislature or the citizens
of the area elect the board members (who are usually
called regents). Boards of Catholic colleges and universities
are usually "advisory" and are constituted in a variety of
ways; they may include representatives of the church hierarchy, the religious order sponsoring the institution, and
sometimes the laity.[1]

DESIRABLE QUALIFICATIONS

Board members come from all levels and segments of
our society. The majority, however, come from the upper
and middle classes—economically, intellectually and so-
cially. They come from these favored classes simply because they have the qualifications that the higher institutions need, or think they need.

The traditional practice in private institutions has been to emphasize the qualification of wealth. Feeling the financial pinch ever since their founding, these institutions quite properly think that trustees should be able to influence the flow of dollars—their own or another's—to the college or university.

The traditional practice in the state institutions has been to favor the qualification of regents candidates from the "right" political party. The administration in power usually wishes to perpetuate itself and its ideals (whether Republican or Democrat), and, naturally, leans toward regents of like mind.

These traditional practices, while generally operative, are not always followed. Frequently, private institutions will nominate a professional person or even a tradesman, who is not rich and has no access to money. Frequently a public institution will find on its board a person with political views quite opposed to the appointing authority. A well-balanced board will have members from various professional and occupational fields, not alone to provide different perspectives, but to provide specialized advice and assistance with diverse problems. In fact, as the collegiate institutions grow and their operations become extensive (both geographically and professionally) it is imperative that boards be composed of a broad range of persons representing many and varied backgrounds.

Among the desirable qualifications listed by most authorities in the field are the following:

1. A college education
2. An active interest in the institution
3. A genuine interest in higher education

4. Ability to attend meetings and work on behalf of the institution
5. Reasonable economic stability
6. A good reputation in business or professional life
7. A good reputation in the community for sound character
   and moral judgment

Since these qualifications are found in the men who control business, finance and industry in this nation, these men
constitute a high percentage of trustees. Over the years,
the percentage of board members from the different occupational groups has varied greatly. It is logical to anticipate
that such variations and changes will continue to occur.
Indeed, it appears salutary that no single occupational or
professional group should remain in the dominant majority
indefinitely. There are few boards, if any, that have at any
given time a perfect balance of occupations or professions.
This supports the contention that boards are not broadly
representative.[2] As long as businessmen, bankers and law-
yers numerically dominate college and university boards
of trustees, the institutions governed by these boards will
feel the influence and effect, directly or indirectly, of these
economically oriented groups.

It appears that the dominant group in a society controls
the social institutions, including those in higher education.
This might make for lopsided representation at any given
time. However, current methods of board operation allow
for shifts in the controlling group as changes occur in the
power complex in society at large. Today businessmen hold
the balance of power on boards of trustees, but, as history
indicates, clergymen held this same position a century ago.[3]

New trustees are usually selected by those already serving on the board, thus providing a self-perpetuating body,

especially in private institutions. Frequently, the alumni select a few board members. In tax-supported institutions, the selection is normally made by the chief executive of the taxing area.

RECRUITMENT AND ELECTION OR APPOINTMENT

Potential trustees after being identified, generally have to be recruited, "sold," or otherwise convinced that they should accept membership on the board. Occasionally such a qualified person will eagerly seek affiliation with a college or university, but usually those wanting a trusteeship are not qualified for it.

Election or appointment to the board of a collegiate institution is a high honor. With this honor go certain responsibilities. While many leaders in the community like the prestige attached to the trusteeship, they shy away from the notion that some time and effort is involved. Most institutions are willing to admit that experience has proven the futility of having as trustees "big names" who do "little work." This misfortune sometimes occurs because the electing body, or the appointing authority, fails to explain to the trustee candidate just what will be expected of him. This is an inexcusable oversight.

When the candidate is selected and agrees to serve, he should be elected or appointed promptly. In the private institutions, such elections are usually made by the full board of trustees. With increasing frequency, alumni organizations are allowed to elect one or two members to the institutional board. In the public institutions, elevation to the board usually occurs by appointment and such appointments are usually made by the chief executive of the taxing body sponsoring the institution. For the city college boards, it is the Mayor; for the state university boards, it is the Governor; for the federal institutions (*i.e.*, the Military, Naval and Air Force Academies), it is the President.

GENERAL ORIENTATION

It is erroneous to assume that simply because a trustee sits on a corporate board of directors, or is a brilliant professional man, or is a staff member of another university, he is (upon election) automatically and immediately prepared to serve as an enlightened trustee. Even if he has served as a trustee in another institution, he may not know enough about his new institution to operate at optimum effectiveness. In virtually every instance, it is incumbent upon the trustee to welcome orientation, education and training.

It is clear from the expressed opinion of trustees and college administrators that a genuine need exists for more and better orientation of trustees. From 45 collegiate institutions questioned on this point, the following response was obtained for presentation to the 1957 Trustee Conference held at Portland State College, Oregon:

	(*Yes*)	(*No*)	(*No reply*)
Are your trustees:			
(a) oriented or trained	8	32	5
(b) if not, would such prove helpful	18	7	20

Experienced trustees and administrative officers have a heavy responsibility to provide adequate "training" for new trustees in this important function. Cowley observes that, "the most important problem in the administration of a college is a clear understanding of the proper relations that should exist between the board of trustees, the president, the faculty, and the students."[4] The understanding of the role and relationships of the various groups within the institution is essential to efficient and harmonious operations.

This orientation has been carried on in several institutions by presidents and other administrative officers. It is usually accomplished before or after board meetings as a regularly scheduled event for new board members. In addition to such discussion sessions, tours of the campus, meetings with faculty and students, and the reading of pertinent publications are encouraged.

THE NEED FOR ORIENTATION

There is a definite need for trustee indoctrination. Unless board members are adequately oriented to their task, it is unlikely that they will perform at maximum effectiveness. Even if properly oriented, there exists the possibility that they will not be effective. Ruml underscores these points by observing that,

The individual trustees often come to their positions with little knowledge of the institution or of higher education and require much careful educating. They may not take their responsibilities too seriously, failing to attend meetings, engaging in long digressions within the meetings, or attempting to hold the meeting at some place other than at the college.

. . . trustees will spend hours looking at the roof of the buildings but not leave any time in which to meet members of the faculty or the students. To an extent, this is the fault of the president who thus directs their attention—and sometimes deliberately— for the sake of keeping them occupied. The trustees do need to become educated about and concerned with the basic educational program, because it is their job to see that the institution is adequately nourished and sufficient provision is made for the facilities and staff. They must know what the institution is about if they are to do this job intelligently.[5]

SPECIFICS OF ORIENTATION

Trustee orientation is attempted in several ways. Some colleges schedule special sessions for new trustees before or after board meetings; some have weekend retreats annually; others set aside a day each month for an "information seminar." Usually the chairman and president conduct these *intra*-institutional sessions, but sometimes senior administrators and senior faculty members are brought in. Where special training sessions for trustees have been offered on an *inter*-institutional basis, in many instances (*e.g.*, Harvard University, University of Chicago, University of Oregon) they are sponsored by a major university, paid for by a foundation, and conducted by national association executives, university administrators or professors of higher education.

Trustee orientation sessions frequently include reference to the history and tradition, aims and goals, organization and administration, problems and potentialities of the institution. For example, in providing orientation for the trustees on New York University's Board for Development, discussion was held on the history of the institution in its community, its aim in claiming to be a private university in the public service, the organizational relationship of the various facets of the university, and some of the academic problems (as well as financial) faced by the institution. At Reed College, the trustee orientation program emphasized the tradition of impeccable scholarship, the goal of maintaining small classes and achieving high quality results, the close integration and rapport between faculty and students, and the necessity for the institution to maintain academic excellence.

Rauh suggests as fundamental items that every trustee should know about his college or university the following: "The basic purposes and traditions of the institution; provisions of charter, by-laws, or collegiate statutes; size of endowment; total operating budget; number of students; number of teaching faculty; faculty salary scales; faculty and employee benefits; facts relating to admission of students including number of applications received; extent and nature of research activities; program of financial assistance to students; composition of student body including geographic distribution and academic background; nature and adequacy of plant and services."[6] I concur with Rauh that the above facts are desirable. However, this list is extensive, and experience at Reed and New York University indicated the value of limiting the subjects covered in trustee orientation to those of greatest interest and imporance (*i.e.*, traditions, philosophy, organizational relationships, budgetary problems, and educational potentialities) of the institution.

FROM ORIENTATION TO ACTION

Every institution should keep its trustees oriented and informed throughout their terms. Much of this continuing education is inculcated by publications on the college or university. Bell wisely recommends that, in addition to keeping board members continuously informed, they should be kept constructively active:

Keep your trustees as fully informed as you can without burying them in reading matter. Tell them the bad news as well as the good—I have found administrations prone to tell us how good we are but to forget how good the competition is. Work your trustees and work them hard. Have them meet as often as possible. Put them on committees. Ask them to do special jobs. It is human nature to think *most* of the things one has worked on. Such activity also teaches trustees what colleges and universities are for. It may even make them want to give you some money. It certainly makes them feel what we all want them to feel, that they are truly part of the great adventure of higher education.[7]

Having been properly oriented, the new trustee is, or should be, ready to work. As part of his orientation he should become acquainted with the organization, mechanics, and procedures of his board. The next chapter covers these subjects and outlines the structural pattern used by the typical college or university board to achieve an orderly and effective utilization of the interests and efforts of board members.

DOCUMENTATION AND COMMENTARY

[1] Harold W. Dodds, *The Academic President—Educator or Caretaker,* New York: McGraw-Hill Company, 1962, p. 211.

[2] Hubert P. Beck, *Men Who Control Our Universities,* New York: King's Crown Press, 1947, p. 151.

[3] Although reference is made to the male as the typical trustee, there is every reason to believe that the distaff side of society has significant contributions to make as board members. Indeed, most women's colleges and co-educational institutions have over the years counted heavily on their female trustees.

[4] William H. Cowley, "The College President As A Leader," *Association of American Colleges Bulletin,* December 1931, p. 546.

[5] Beardsley Ruml and Donald H. Morrison, *Memo to a College Trustee,* N.Y.: McGraw-Hill Book Company, 1959, p. 229.

[6] Morton A. Rauh, *College and University Trusteeship,* Yellow Springs, Ohio: The Antioch Press, 1959, p. 86.

[7] Laird Bell, "From the Trustee's Corner," originally a talk at the University of Chicago, June 1956.

6 ORGANIZATION OF BOARDS OF TRUSTEES

Just as there are no two identical colleges, there are no two boards that operate in exactly the same fashion ... at least I have found no twins among the more than 500 institutions affiliated in the Independent College Funds of America. This is understandable because of the shades of difference between the institutions and among the individuals who serve them as trustees.

SIZE AND TYPES OF BOARDS

Since the size of governing boards varies from approximately 5 to 100, and since there are more than 2,000 institutions in America, it has been estimated that there are approximately 30,000 trustees in this nation.[1] If this is correct, then the average board of trustees is composed of 15 members.

With the exception of a few Ivy League institutions, there is one governing board for each private institution and they all operate on a unicameral basis. There are a few large urban universities where a secondary board has been established, but generally these are for specific purposes and are considered *ad hoc* (such as the former Board for Development at New York University). Many Catholic colleges and universities have boards of *advisors,* usually composed of laymen, that assist the churchmen. In some states where there are two or more tax-supported institutions, there is a single board that governs all such institutions.

BASIC ORGANIZATION

The fundamental structure of a college or university board is not unlike that of a business organization. It has officers to provide leadership, rules under which to operate, and a traditional pattern that guides its activities. With the exception of some very small boards that always function as a committee-of-the-whole, most boards utilize a committee structure. In addition, there are regular meeting dates and places agreed upon normally at the beginning of each academic, fiscal or calendar year.

The officers of the board are the chairman, vice chairman, secretary and treasurer. They are ordinarily elected for an indefinite period, but occasionally they are elected on an annual or biannual basis. The role of the chairman is to preside, give leadership and inspiration, and serve as the senior member of the corporation. He should be a man well endowed with free time, energy, intelligence, devotion to the institution, and ability to lead his fellow trustees. In his absence, it is the vice chairman who heads the board, and this person needs many of the same sterling qualities.

The secretary of the board is the person legally responsible for its record keeping. However, most boards have a stenographer present at all regular meetings to assist the secretary with the minutes and other details. The treasurer of the board is the person legally responsible for its fiscal and financial operations. Frequently, the same person serves as treasurer of the board and of the institution. Invariably he is assisted by the chief business and financial officer of the college or university.[2]

COMMITTEE STRUCTURE

There are three major areas of board operation, plus several important and related functions. To keep the work of the board moving smoothly, committees are appointed in these areas and for these special functions. There are several reasons for using committees:

1. They accomplish more in less time than could the full board
2. They encourage intimate contact with the problems of the institution
3. They utilize the specialized skills of individual trustees more readily
4. They provide for closer relationships between trustees and faculty
5. They enable small groups to meet locally with greater frequency than the full board

The first major area is that of the *academic*. Since this is the most important sector of the institution's program, it is logical that the board would have one or more committees functioning in this area. There is wide disagreement about the role of the trustees in this facet; this will be discussed in detail subsequently. Committees are identified

by different names in different schools, although they may
have the same responsibility. For example, the chief trustees group in this area is called the educational affairs committee, or the academic committee, or the curriculum committee. In larger institutions with bigger boards, there are
frequently other committees charged with the functional
considerations that their titles indicate; trustees committee
on faculty, on students, on alumni, on athletics, on honorary
degrees, on the library. Harvard and Chicago offer interesting examples of such committee structure.

The second major area of the boards consideration is that
of *finance*. There is little or no disagreement about the pri-
macy of the trustee's role in this area. Here the board member is generally very much "at home" and his practical experience in business or the professions is valued highly.
The main committee is called, quite logically, the finance
committee, and it deals with all, or an assigned part, of the
institution's fiscal and financial operations. Customarily
there are other committees convened in support of this committee and dealing with the matters designated by their
titles; trustees committee on budget, on physical plant (or
buildings and grounds), on endowment (or investments),
on scholarships (and loans). Pittsburgh and Swarthmore
provide illustrations of committees in this area.

The third major area is that of *promotion*. In the private
institutions, this area has become increasingly important
in the last decade. The reasons for this are obvious; the
non-tax-supported institutions, must seek more adequate
levels of financial support; this support must come, at least
in part, from the private sectors of the economy; the trustees, as leaders in the community, are the logical persons
to lead the search to satisfy this need. In the public insti-

tutions, while the need for promotion is not as crucial, it has been found desirable to have certain trustees (or committees of trustees) concern themselves with the committee functions grouped in this area. The main committee is that of development; secondary committees are on public relations, on government relations, on planning, on alumni.[3] N.Y.U. and Reed, for similar reasons, developed unique groups of trustees in promotional affairs.

SPECIAL COMMITTEES

Besides the committees in the three major areas of the board's concern there are other groups of considerable significance that deserve special mention.

The *executive committee* is the pivotal group in the hierarchy of the board's structure.[4] It is usually composed of the officers and key board members. As a rule, it meets more frequently than the board and has specific authority delegated to it. Like all other committees, it reports back to the board, but such action as it takes (especially between board meetings) is quickly ratified. Sometimes this committee is composed of board members residing near the institution or the main city in its state. This geographical grouping is especially helpful where the board is large and scattered through a state, region or the nation.

The *presidential search committee* is typically composed of key trustees and is appointed on an *ad hoc* basis when the need for its function arises. Frequently faculty members are invited to sit with this trustee committee. Sometimes the chairman and other officers serve in this group. Its job is to take the magnificent (but usually unattainable) presidential description provided by the board, seek out the men described, screen them carefully, and ascertain if they will serve the institution. This committee is wise to secure helpful suggestions or nominations from all possible sources, including the board, the administration, the faculty, the alumni, the foundations, and the major universities of the nation. When it has found one or more such presidential candidates, their names are turned over to the board for scheduled interviews. Usually it is the full board that elects the president.

The *trustee nominating committee* is the group which proposes new trustees to the board. It is charged with the task of filling vacancies with the best men available. The matter of selection has been outlined in the previous chapter.

One of the responsibilities of the board is to serve as a court of last resort. For this reason an *ad hoc grievance committee* is sometimes formed to adjudicate disputes arising on campus. While faculty and students should have the majority of their problems solved by the administration, a grievance committee can prove a helpful safety valve at certain critical periods.[5]

The next three chapters will deal in detail with the standing committees in the three major areas of the board's concern. The method of appointing committee members, the qualifications of such members, their function and tenure will be discussed subsequently.

MEETINGS OF THE BOARD

Governing boards meet at various intervals, usually on a set schedule announced well in advance of the first meeting. These intervals vary from weekly to annually with the bi-monthly meeting being most common.

Where the board is very large, or scattered across the

nation, the meetings are infrequent, possibly annually or semi-annually. In these instances the executive, or local advisory committee meets monthly or at least quarterly.

Boards, and to some extent committees, tend to meet in one of three places: (1) on campus, (2) in the college town, (3) in the nearest large city where the most members reside. Board meetings vary in length from an hour to several days, depending upon the frequency of meetings and the pressure of business.

Committee meetings occur more often than board meetings. They are normally held between or just before meetings at which the committee's deliberations are reported. These groups usually meet in the place geographically most convenient to the majority.[6]

MODUS OPERANDI

As in any board or committee meeting, the chairman generally presides. Prior to the meeting, he and the president formulate an agenda for the meeting. In the absence of the chairman, the vice chairman or another officer of the board will preside. It is seldom that the president occupies the chair; the University of Colorado is one exception.

Depending on the kind of people involved, the meeting is moved along by the chairman or the president. At times, the president will have certain administrative officers, senior faculty members, or other guests on hand to serve as resource people on special questions.

The primary function of the governing board is to determine the broad policies under which the institution operates. However, this determination of policy seldom takes place without the professional leadership of the institution, notably the president, playing an active role.

The board in framing its edicts expects the president to share the initiative; relies heavily on the president's approval; follows his suggestions in determining academic sentiment or university needs; makes awards or dismissals in accordance with his verdicts; agrees upon what shall be done first and what last and what not at all, largely according to his judgment or preference.

The governing board alone cannot be expected to develop all the policies that it should adopt as control measures over the operations of the institution. All it can do is lend its judgment to the policies that have been developed and proposed for it by the administration. But, the fact remains that the board cannot officially delegate the responsibility for the president taking all the initiative. Perhaps the best approach is suggested in "Burns' Law," that the most effective administration and governance occurs in direct proportion to the amount of mutual influence, cooperative effort and shared initiative between president and board.

FUTURE ORGANIZATION

The role of the trustee is increasing in importance.[7] As the role matures, and as new trustees are enlisted, it is incumbent upon experienced trustees (especially the chairman) and senior administrators (especially the president) to provide them with (1) inspiration and enthusiasm by example, (2) initial and continuing orientation to the job, and (3) efficient and effective committee structure within which they can make their maximum contribution. This latter point deserves amplification.

Most boards are not as effective or as efficient as they could (and should) be. One reason for this situation is that their *modus operandi* and committee structure are archaic.

Few scholars of college administration and governance have taken time to examine carefully the past and present conditions of the board's function and coordination. In consequence, patterns used a century ago, or found desirable in industry, are still in use. Education, particularly higher education, is a dynamic entity and its governance should reflect this. Higher education should take some "calculated risks," seek enlightened leadership, encourage progressive ideas, and accept new operational channels.[8] Moribund thinking and outmoded operations on the part of its boards and committees can no longer be tolerated. Granted that there is no one way to govern an institution, and allowing that all colleges and universities are different, nevertheless it is possible to suggest improvements and innovations which can be applied to any institution.

One such new device is illustrated in the proposed organization chart for a large university board. It recommends the board establish standing committees in its three major areas, and that these be composed of the chairmen of the sub-committees under each of these areas. It suggests that all board members serve on one of the sub-committees, and, when needed, some trustees be appointed to serve on the special or *ad hoc* committees (such as trustee nomination, presidential search and grievance committees). The executive committee would be comprised of the officers, plus the chairmen of the three standing committees. The president of the institution would be an ex-officio member of the board, executive committee and three standing committees. He would deputize his academic vice president to represent him with the trustees' academic affairs committee, his business vice president to represent him with the trustees' financial committee, and his development

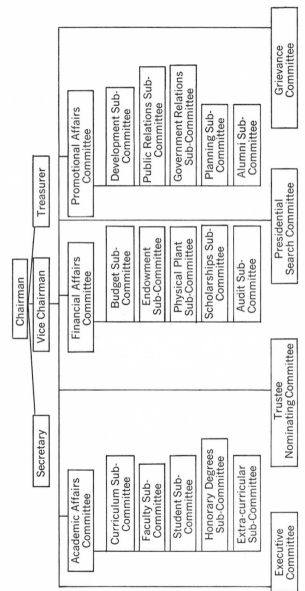

**ORGANIZATION CHART FOR
A LARGE UNIVERSITY BOARD OF TRUSTEES**

vice president to represent him with the trustees' promotional committee.

The virtue of this plan is that it can press into effective service, with satisfying committee assignments, up to one hundred trustees. The service would be *effective* because leadership interaction and channels of communication would be clear and logical. The assignments would be *satisfying* because each standing committee would have top administrative staff assistance and the sub-committees would be smalll enough to allow every member full expression in deliberation.

DOCUMENTATION AND COMMENTARY

[1] There is no single source or agency where full, current, and accurate statistics and information on trustees can be obtained. With interest in the trusteeship mounting, the establishment of such a source or agency might constitute a foundation project of transcendent importance. The Trustees of the Carnegie Foundation for the Advancement of Teaching recently published the results of an "all-day discussion of the role of the college and university trustees." This unusual document states that "boards of colleges and universities vary in size from 3 to 115, with a median of 15."

[2] Harold Dodds, *The Academic President—Educator or Caretaker*, New York: McGraw-Hill Book Company, 1962, p. 94.

[3] John A. Pollard, *Fund-Raising for Higher Education*, New York: Harper and Row, 1958, p. 89.

[4] Morton R. Rauh, *College and University Trusteeship*, Yellow Springs, Ohio: The Antioch Press, 1959, p. 73.

[5] If the problem is sufficiently critical, the board is well advised to approach it as a committee-of-the-whole.

[6] Harold Stoke, *The American College President*, New York: Harper and Row, 1959, p. 55.

[7] The writer's Ph.D. dissertation, on file at New York University, dealt with the facts proving this hypothesis.

[8] Dodds, *op. cit.*, p. 262.

7 RESPONSIBILITY FOR ACADEMIC AFFAIRS

As the first of the three major areas in which trustee committees operate, academic affairs deserves greater consideration than it has received in the past. There has been little information available for the trustee who wants concrete answers about his relationship to educational affairs.

GENERAL RESPONSIBILITY

In addition to their general fiduciary functions, trustees have specific responsibilities to the president, the faculty and the students to guarantee that the college or university will be what it purports to be, will fulfill its contractual obligations, and will continue in perpetuity as a reputable collegiate institution. In effect, the board has the moral as well as legal responsibility for the kind and extent of educational programs provided.

THE FORMULATION OF POLICY

Trustees exercise their rights and obligations in this area by formulating the educational policy under which the institution operates. The board cannot formulate policy in a vacuum, so it must have (through its educational committees) close contact with the academic program. This contact should be designed to provide all the information that the board will need.

When the board, and especially the educational committees, hear reports on the academic program these should receive careful consideration and evaluation. If the program as reported fulfills all the provisions of the charter aims of the institution, there is no remedial action necessary. However, education is not static; it is ever changing, and modifications must frequently be effected in even the finest academic programs. Consequently, the board must weigh *what is being done* with *what should be done*—and take appropriate action.

Board members are generally more objective about institutional programs than are members of the staff or faculty. First, they are off-campus and in the community; secondly, they are not involved in the day-to-day operation; thirdly, they see the total institutional program, not a single part; fourthly, they are laymen or generalists without allegiance to a scholarly discipline or department; fifthly, they know the needs (occupational and professional) of the community served; sixthly, they know the public sentiment and reactions to the institution and its programs. For these, and other reasons, trustees are in a favorable position to ask pertinent questions, make practical proposals, argue from sound perspectives, and decide upon policies that react to the best interest of the institution, the community and the persons involved.[1]

THE EDUCATIONAL COMMITTEES

Within the domain of academic affairs there is invariably one or more committees at work. These committees always report to the board; they are advisory, not action committees. Among the committees "on education" in a major university might be found the following: curriculum, instruction, faculty, student, honorary degrees, and extracurricular.

The academic affairs committee, or its subcommittees as listed, are responsible for observing, studying and evaluating at first hand the educational operations of the institution. Members of this committee, working through the president or appropriate dean, should be afforded ample opportunity to meet and talk with students and faculty. They should, at certain times, be enabled to visit classes, seminars, laboratory sessions and other operational facets. They should be familiar with the work of the administrators most closely related to the academic program (i.e., the dean of the college, the librarian, the director of admissions, the registrar).

The curriculum committee needs to know some of the details and specifics of the over-all educational picture. It must have certain statistical information upon which to base its deliberations and its reports to the full board. Among the criteria that it can use for evaluative purposes are the following:

1. Ratio of students to faculty
2. Number of courses per faculty member
3. Number of courses offered per year

4. Number of courses enrolling ten or fewer
5. Faculty compensation in dollars per student

Among the members of the committees in this area should be some professional educators. Scholars in this field of administration and governance agree that while there should be some college-connected people on the board, they should not be employes of the institution being governed. Many boards have elected administrators and faculty members from other institutions. When such experts are available they should be invited to serve on the curriculum (or other academic) committee.[2]

RELATIONSHIPS ON CAMPUS

While the board should formulate policy, it should not implement that policy. On a step-by-step basis, a logical approach to securing optimum academic productivity might be as follows: (1) the educational affairs committee observes the academic programs, (2) it secures the advice of deans or senior faculty members, (3) it reports findings and proposals to the board, (4) the board deliberates on these reports and (5) with the advice of the president, it formulates policy.

The faculty should have ample opportunity to influence academic policy. It should, however, not have full authority or responsibility for naming the courses and directing the teachers.

The final decision in any aspect of the institution's operations, including the academic, rests with the trustees. Ruml observes that, "Trustees do have a legal, over-all responsibility that goes much beyond that of the faculties. If the welfare of the college demands it, they should take drastic action—only they have the real power to do it."[3] Faculty should have a strong *voice,* not a strong *vote,* in the determination of academic policy.

The academic dean must have a close relationship and give guidance to the trustee committees in the instructional sphere. He is the executive officer or administrator closest to the education of students and should have a better grasp of the program than even the president. Unfortunately, many academic deans have neglected to maintain an intimate relationship with faculty members and students. They have become armchair strategists, more concerned with academic bookkeeping than with ideas and people. However, reliance must be placed upon the persons closest to the educational program if the board (through its academic committees) is to be kept fully informed.

The president must supplement (for the board) the reports of the academic committees. Although he is concerned with "the big picture," he must have a reasonable degree of accurate knowledge about the curriculum, the faculty and the students, so that he can discuss these matters with the board.

The president and certain other administrative officers frequently are qualified by education, training and experience to exert a major influence in the area of the curriculum. Many of these people have been on the faculty, have developed a broad view of the institution's educational needs, and may have more objectivity than some faculty members. Perkins observes, "It is high time that administration in higher education was recognized for what it is; a vitally necessary function, one of the most difficult of all areas of administrative activity, and an undertaking to be consciously prepared for."[4] Once this recognition occurs, faculty members and administrators will be able to work in closer harmony toward the solution of many of the perplexing problems in higher education.

As a rule, the trustees themselves are not unaware of the curricular and other educational needs of the institution. Some of them are quite conversant about these matters, having contact in the local or national community with other educational agencies. These are the kind of broad-gauged relationships which give them valuable perspectives. In many instances they quickly become knowledgeable about the existing courses, seminars, tutorials and other offerings of their institution.

AUTHORITY AND CONTROL

Although there is little support for his suggestion, Ruml has been widely quoted on the point that trustees should move in and take over the supervision of the curriculum. While the foregoing comments indicate a need for more forthright action on the part of the trustees and the president in curricular matters, it is clear that no single person or group has all the answers in this controversial area. It appears that the faculty still has a strong grip on this matter. Examining arguments on this subject, McGrath raises an interesting point by observing that, "The additional financial resources which will become available to the independent liberal arts colleges from endowments, gifts and increased tuition fees will not be sufficient to put these institutions in a desirable competitive position in obtaining faculty members. Salaries can be raised to an appropriate level only by a more economical management of the curriculum and the more efficient use of staff time."[5]

One of the primary reasons advanced for trustees developing an active interest in the curriculum is centered in finances. The board, rather than the faculty, is by experience better able to know what the institution can (and cannot) afford. This is a sensitive point, and any businessman or industrialist who raises the issue of money as related to academic productivity or educational economics is likely to be confronted with the criticism that he stresses problems of financing more than those of education. It is clear that college trustees and administrators, politicians and bureaucrats should move carefully in this area. However, as Harris admits, "It is my considered opinion that the largest responsibility rests on the faculty, generally most reluctant to cut down on wastes and modify curriculum, teaching hours, and teaching methods."[6]

THE CRUX OF THE CURRICULUM PROBLEM

The curriculum is the sum total of the formal educational program of the institution. Ruml observes, "The curriculum of a liberal college is intended to be its principal instrument for the advancement of liberal education. The choice by the trustees of the collective faculty as the agency for the design and administration of the college's curriculum is a particularly unfortunate one."[7] It is apparent that most trustees do not agree. Actual practices of most institutions sustain faculties in this position of dominating the curriculum.

The basic thesis of Ruml's book is that the Board of Trustees has final responsibility under its charter for the educational program as well as for the property of the institution. Having total authority and responsibility, it also has accountability for a performance it is willing to defend to the state, to the national and local community, to donors, to parents and students, to the individual members of the faculty. The trustees, says Ruml, must take back from the faculty as a body its present authority over the design and administration of the curriculum. But, at its present state of academic knowledge and educational orientation, the typical board is hardly qualified to take over the "design and administration" of the curriculum.

Major curricular decisions should be shared by the trustees, the administration and the faculty. However, many writers feel that this kind of "troika" would be unmanageable because there are already too many areas of compromise. Corson suggests, "The result of this diffusion and decentralization of decision making is often costly. Decisions by faculties regarding educational programs are often the result of compromise among specialists, made without the leavening and stimulating influence of thoughtful leaders of the society who (sometimes) serve on boards of trustees."[8]

There are several arguments or reasons why the faculty should not have exclusive control of the curriculum. Some experts in governance say that the teacher is individualistic in his attitudes toward regulation of educational affairs and that he seems instinctively to resist organized authority when it is concerned with curriculum and teaching. Their contention is that if there must be controls, let the faculty agree that the controls be democratically imposed and administered. Also, in this area, let the administration agree that "that government is best which governs least."

General agreement exists that this is a delicate and difficult matter. This task, in the jargon of management, is called *control* and control is a nasty word in any self-respecting academic community. And, yet, the widely read leaders in the field including certain trustees, administrators *and* faculty members, concur that some kind or measure of control is long overdue if only for the good of the faculty itself. As in any large organization, some centralized leadership is essential. A university is a diverse institution and the typical curriculum is incredibly complex. Sound planning for the future requires central direction and coordination of the various elements of the plan.

TRUSTEES AND STUDENTS

Many pundits, including some trustees, have jokingly remarked that colleges would be wonderful if it were not for the students. But the point made is that the students are an important—perhaps the most important—group on campus. They are sometimes a very difficult group—a fact which many presidents quickly admit.[9]

Recently the field of higher education has been staggered by perhaps the most important and serious problem or threat of the past decade, the "student revolt." While the Berkeley campus of the University of California was the most prominent battleground in 1964-65, examples of this unique revolution were found in many well-known educational quadrangles (e.g., Yale University, St. John's University, Brooklyn College.)

There are several reasons for the student unrest, many ways to cope with it, and many devices for shaping it into a constructive force. History is replete with proof that college students generally can be counted upon to engage in activities that are sometimes "larks", sometimes anti-social, and sometimes downright dangerous.

These kinds of behavioral aberrations may be more prevalent now than in the past because of the pressures resulting from a combination of the "tidal wave" of students and the "explosion of knowledge." As it became necessary for colleges and universities to accommodate more students, it was logical for these institutions to grow larger physically and numerically. As it became necessary for colleges and universities to discover, collate, and transmit vast quantities of new knowledge, it was logical for these institutions to obtain the services of top-flight scientists and scholars, many of whom pledged greater allegiance to research and their discipline than to teaching and their students.

Thus, the factors that brought about this mood of student rebellion were bigness and impersonality, lack of concern for students, faculty neglect of students, mounting academic pressures, and excessive paternalism. These fostered in the students a lack of institutional loyalty, a sense of growing power, an urge to play a dominant role, and a frustration with regard to their academic programs.

There are no simple explanations on how to cope with this serious situation in higher education. However, the most obvious solution may be the best—decentralize into smaller units. No reasonable professor of higher education, academic administrator, or experienced trustee advocates going all the way back to the primitive concept of the teacher and pupil seated on the same log. But, every reasonable educational leader will accept the dictum that the first responsibility of the schools, colleges and universities is to teach.

When that logical dictum is disregarded, a major facet of education is ignored. Granted that a great state university has three main functions—teaching, research and service— teaching and learning must come first. The student must not become, as President Logan Wilson of the American

Council on Education warns, "the forgotten man" on campus.

It would be incorrect to imply that student unrest is always limited to large universities, or that every small liberal arts college does a better teaching job. Such generalizations are fatuous. But, it is true that in most instances there are closer student-faculty and student-trustee relationships, plus greater emphasis on teaching (rather than faculty research and consulting) in the smaller, private institutions.

Thus, among the ways to minimize serious student revolts is to establish smaller collegiate units for undergraduates—such as President Robert Burns has done so successfully with his "cluster college" concept at the University of the Pacific. Another way to cope with this problem is to employ more teachers and fewer researchers, consultants and clinicians. A third method is to recognize that students need and deserve greater opportunity to participate as young adults in the affairs of their institution, its community, this nation, and the world. Board members can contribute to this third method, especially on an extra-mural basis.

At the graduate level, there is every reason for large universities to emphasize research and service, along with teaching. This is especially true of the urban universities supported by city or state funds. These institutions must continue to remain in the vanguard and at the cutting edge of our society in discovering new truths and applying this information to the needs of their communities.

At the undergraduate level, there is every reason for the small colleges to emphasize teaching and student growth (intellectually, physically and morally). This is especially true of the private residential colleges supported by tuition and gifts. These institutions must continue to teach students to think clearly, to reason wisely, and to act humanely. As experience over the last 800 years has proven at Oxford and Cambridge, it is possible to have small residential colleges for proper teaching and supervised living within and a part of a great university.

It is time that members of governing boards, as well as professional educators, took the necessary steps to minimize further demonstrations. Such steps should include efforts designed to channel the enormous energies, tremendous enthusiasm, and emergent idealism of our students into constructive pursuits of seminal value to them, to the institutions and to society (in that sequence).

TRUSTEES AND FACULTY

It is appropriate that careful consideration be given the relationship between the faculty and the trustees. As mentioned earlier, the trustees need a closer, stronger relationship to the curriculum. They can achieve this best by establishing better *rapport* with the faculty. Bell has said, "Furthermore, the trustees cannot properly abdicate *all* concern with educational matters. Logically the trustees, as the controlling body, have the right—and in fact the duty—to determine what *kind* of education shall be offered."[10] The trustees should not delve into the details of curriculum construction and academic scheduling. Rather, the boards should make certain that the quality and quantity of the academic offering provide the kind and extent of education that the charter, traditions and catalogue purport to provide. This kind of governance is understandable to faculty members and will be appreciated by them. Actually, both the board and the faculty should develop for each other a large measure of admiration and respect.

Sometimes this desirable rapport and its resulting cooperation between faculty and governing board can be brought about through an able and energetic president bridging the gap. Some trustees hold that the president is a businessman riding firm but gentle herd on an interesting aggregation of seals. Actually the president should be the first member of the faculty, and essentially its leader in general educational policy. Leonard underscores this view, saying, "In matters relating to the technical phases of educational policy, it is obviously good judgment for the board to accept expert advice which it may reasonably expect from the chief administrative officer, or members of his staff, through him."[11] If this idea is widely accepted, it then becomes essential that the president not only be a sound academician, but have close rapport with his faculty on behalf of the board of trustees.

DOCUMENTATION AND COMMENTARY

[1] The several trustees serving as "collaborators" in this study were unanimous in their feeling that the *objectivity* of the board members was one of the most important reasons for having lay leaders, or at least "off campus" people, as college trustees.

[2] Harold W. Dodds, *The Academic President—Educator or Caretaker,* New York: McGraw-Hill Company, 1962, p. 225

[3] Beardsley Ruml and Donald Morrison, *Memo to a College Trustee,* New York: McGraw-Hill Company, 1959, p. 227

[4] John A. Perkins, "Public Administration and the College Administrator," *Harvard Educational Review,* No. 4, 1955, p. 25

[5] Earl J. McGrath, *Memo to a College Faculty Member,* New York: Teachers College, Columbia University, 1961, p. 53

[6] Seymour E. Harris, *Higher Education: Resources and Finance,* New York: McGraw-Hill Company, 1962, p. 557

[7] Ruml, *op. cit.,* p. 7. It is interesting that during the writer's (G.P.B.) visits to approximately 200 institutions of higher education and discussion with several hundred faculty members, many of the latter agreed with Ruml's contention for an enormous variety of reasons.

[8] John J. Corson, *Governance of Colleges and Universities,* New York: McGraw Hill Book Company, 1960, p. 25

[9] John S. Brubacher and Willis Rudy, *Higher Education in Transition,* Harper and Row, 1958, p. 338

[10] Laird Bell, "From the Trustee's Corner", originally a talk at the University of Chicago, June, 1956.

[11] R. J. Leonard, E. S. Evenden, F. B. O'Rear, and others, *Survey of Higher Education for the United Lutheran Church in America,* New York: Teachers College, 1929, p. 84

<table>
<tr><td>8</td><td>RESPONSIBILITY FOR
BUDGET AND FINANCE</td></tr>
</table>

Boards of trustees were first formed to assist the president and professors of the early colleges in handling the business interests of their institutions. Since 1636 this aspect of the institutions' operations has in many instances, become big business. Harvard's endowment (book value) now exceeds $1,000,000,000, the operations budget of the University of California is about $700,000,000, the physical plant of New York University is valued in excess of $100,000,000. The magnitude of these figures underscores the need for astute advice and assistance from the trustees in formulating wise policies pertaining to budgeting, finance, business and plant management.

GENERAL RESPONSIBILITY

The responsibility of the board is complete in dealing with financial affairs and the physical plant. This responsibility and accountability is shared by the president, to a lesser extent. With the help of the chief business officer, the president is expected to operate the organization efficiently, effectively and economically. He need not always balance the budget; but he should have a logical explanation for the board when it does not balance.

FORMULATION OF POLICY

The board must decide upon the kind of financial and business practices that will be employed at its institution. There is no set pattern that can be applied to these operations in colleges and universities across the nation. Even institutions of the same size and type, because of differences in staff or location, will function under quite different policies.

To a large extent, the board will go along with the traditional pattern of business management it has inherited. As changes are needed, it will normally expect one of its trustee committees, or the president, to present well-thought-out proposals. Boards are inherently conservative and higher education is inherently liberal; consequently, some problems arise in terms of the necessity for innovations.

There are several functions in the sphere of college or university business management. For that reason, in all but the smallest colleges, there is usually more than one trustee committee deliberating, studying, evaluating, analyzing, advising and reporting on the business and financial operations. The typical university might have the following committees (or sub-committees): budget, investment or endowment, physical plant or buildings and grounds, scholarship and student aid.

In order to provide for the smooth functioning of these

groups, the trustee's operational or organizational chart in Chapter VI might be followed. This calls for an overall finance committee composed of the chairman of four or five related sub-committees and staff service provided by the chief business officer. The chairman of the finance committee would then be a member of the executive committee of the board.

THE FINANCE COMMITTEE

In the case of the small college with a board varying from eight to twelve members, it is desirable to have a single committee in the area of business affairs. When such is the practice, it is called the finance committee and its purview includes the numerous functions allocated to other committees (or sub-committees) as indicated on the organization chart for the more complex institution and/or a larger governing board. When there is a single committee operating in this area, the function of planning and budgeting usually reverts back to the full board.

The trustees assigned in this area must be carefully selected for their interest (if not experience) in this important activity. Since a preponderance of trustees are businessmen, it is easy to secure qualified people for such assignments. But, even though they may be experienced in business, financial and industrial management in the community, since colleges and universities operate outside the profit motive, they will find educational institutions using practices somewhat at variance with their own. For this reason, adequate orientation must be provided for all trustees— orientation emphasizing both the similarities and differences between the colleges and the corporations.[1]

THE BUDGET COMMITTEE

If a separate trustees' group is assigned to budgetary considerations, it is usually related to the business and financial area of the institution's program. However, since the annual budget is in effect a fiscal statement of the institution's educational program, it is closely connected to the academic area. Then too, since funds must be raised to cover estimated expenses of the budget, there exists a link between it and the development area.

Generally the president, with the help of his chief business and financial officer, discusses the proposed income and expenses, problems and potentialities with the budget committee well in advance of the meeting at which the full board will consider the annual budget. Frequently the board chairman and the treasurer will sit in on these preliminary hearings. After the budget committee has carefully considered the statement, it is presented to the full board for further consideration and ultimate adoption.

Some colleges and universities utilize long-term budgets, occasionally spanning up to twenty years, for planning purposes. These are particularly effective for capital projections and future fund-raising campaigns. Annual budget forecasts are recognized as essential in revealing trends that might otherwise pass unnoticed.

THE PHYSICAL PLANT COMMITTEE

This committee (or sub-committee) is frequently referred to as the building and grounds committee. As the title indicates, this group of trustees is concerned with the facilities of the college or university. Their deliberations should be centered around the objective of providing an attractive

and effective physical environment in which the educational program will flourish.

Among the major problems these trustees will face are
maintenance, utilities, landscaping, building modification,
new construction, fire prevention, traffic control and campus planning. In large, private universities with extensive
holdings in real estate, these trustees are sometimes asked
to provide advice and guidance on acquisition, operation,
and disposal. Often there are on the board persons of great
ability in the matters mentioned above; certainly they
should serve on this committee. Their knowledge and wisdom based upon broad practical experience, can be of in-
estimable help to educational administrators who are usually lacking in this kind of training.[2]

THE INVESTMENT COMMITTEE

This group is alternatively entitled the endowment committee. Few publicly supported colleges or universities
have large endowments. Consequently, committees or sub-
committees functioning in this precinct are found chiefly
in the privately supported institutions.

The older and larger universities have traditionally received substantial support as yield from endowment. The
endowment consists of capital given for investment from
which income is expected to flow *ad infinitum* to the institution. It is the responsibility of the board to invest wisely
and to supervise carefully the institution's portfolio in order to secure the best possible return commensurate with
prudent investment procedures. The board is usually too
large to be intimately familiar with the investment program. It therefore delegates a portion of its responsibilities
in this realm to an investment committee, or sub-commit-

tee, which in turn coordinates closely with outside professional counsel. The trustees group serving in this fiduciary facet of the board's function, normally is composed of trust officers, investment analysts, brokers, and other principal figures who are knowledgeable about securities.

In recent years there has been serious criticism of the investment policies of educational institutions indicating that they are overly conservative. While trustees should guard against investing in highly speculative issues, they should be cognizant of their responsibility to place the endowment funds in securities where capital appreciation and/or yield is better than average.

THE SCHOLARSHIP COMMITTEE

Some disagreement exists as to the need for a group of trustees on the board to act as a committee or sub-committee concerned with such related matters as student aid, scholarships and loans. In the public colleges and universities, where there is little or no tuition, the need for board consideration of these items may be slight or even non-existent. However, in the private institutions, with tuitions constantly rising, there appears to be a need for periodic evaluation of and modification in the policies dealing with financial help to students. As tuition is increased scholarships, loans and other forms of aid should also be increased. While the administrators (especially the chief financial officer, the vice president or dean of students and the directors of admissions) giving professional leadership in this province should help the president formulate recommendations, there should be some trustees familiar with these problems and available to provide advice and guidance in developing board policy for their solution.[3]

This is a functional domain where female trustees might make significant contributions. Then too, recent graduates and young alumni on the board are in a position to evaluate the needs of the students within the limitations of the budget. And, finally, if there are previous scholarship recipients on the board, they should serve with this group.

THE AUDIT COMMITTEE

Because committees operating in this area bear (for the board) a heavy responsibility for the financial health of the institution, there have been convened at times in many colleges and universities, committees or sub-committees on audit and accounting. These are "watchdog" groups and are usually formed when particular problems have arisen. Most institutions of higher education, like their counterparts in business, have an outside or independent audit conducted annually. The report of audit is usually presented by the president (or chief financial officer) to the finance committee (or the full board) for approval, acceptance and adoption.

Since the majority of the chief business and financial officers appear to be competent, and since most institutions have good internal accounting as well as an external audit, governing boards have not normally concerned themselves with the details of who directs or how the audit is conducted; their primary (and rightful) concern has been the diagnosis of the institution's fiscal condition as charted by the official audit.

THE EDUCATIONAL BALANCE SHEET

It is no simple task for trustees untrained in academic affairs immediately to comprehend how and why colleges and universities can, and sometimes should, operate in a deficit position. Briefly, the "how" is answered by the proven facts that there is no necessity for an educational institution to show a profit or surplus. Indeed, if it does show an excess of income over expenses for an extended number of years, it is not providing the quantity or quality of education expected of it. Obviously, large deficits cannot be tolerated indefinitely, as a day of reckoning is bound to come. But, as long as there are reserves and resources that can be called upon, an occasional annual deficit is acceptable.

The "why" of deficit operations is explained by similar pragmatic experience. It is the first and major responsibility of every educational institution to expend the maximum amount of money possible for its educational program. Although the institution is normally expected to live within its income, it is better occasionally to exceed income rather than water-down academic offerings. Since it is illegal for public institutions to exceed their budgets, many have resorted to high powered fund drives to obtain the additional revenue needed.

It is the difficult job of the board to compare the financial balance sheet with the educational balance sheet. The guiding of this intellectual exercise calls for ingenuity on the part of the president and his top administrators, and for patient and sympathetic understanding by the board.

INFLUENCE AND EFFECT

Many persons inside and outside of higher education feel that the trustees and administrators easily "manipulate" the budget in order to secure desired changes in the educational program. In part, their feeling is correct; certainly the budget exerts a major influence on the curriculum. But, casual manipulation is limited because a major portion of expenses are fixed charges, the usual margin between income and expenses is too slim to encourage extensive budgetary maneuvering. Unless an unexpected windfall occurs, the resources with which to undertake new projects are seldom available.[4]

Although geared to the future, the budget must reflect the continuance of the desirable academic traditions of the past. Any attempt to ignore these traditions (honors courses, special seminars, etc.) in the budget would end in chaos. For example, comparisons with earlier experiences, both financial and academic, provide opportunities for identifying and evaluating expenditures rising or decreasing at unusual rates. The fact that the budget is a flexible financial instrument that must be reviewed periodically, and formally adopted annually, makes it a valuable mirror for reflecting on the past, evaluating the present, and especially planning for the future. Although influenced by faculty pressures and operated by the administration, the budget is still the central control available to the trustees. Its effect on the institution is enormous.[5]

PRIVATE VERSUS PUBLIC ACCOUNTABILITY

In the private institutions, the budget is approved and adopted by the governing board, and the board must then ensure that the estimated receipts (from tuition, endowment, gifts, grants and government) are obtained. In the public institutions, the budget adopted by the board must be taken one step further; it must be approved and receipts appropriated for it by the responsible taxing body (in the city, county, state or federal government).

This simply means that the trustees of the independent-
ly supported colleges and universities have greater freedom of operations and greater responsibility for fund-raising. The private institutions are directly beholden to no
one; at least in theory, they can offer any combination of
courses for which money can be raised. The public institutions are directly beholden to the appropriating authority; at least in theory, they must offer the combination of
courses for which money will be appropriated.

EDUCATIONAL COST ACCOUNTING

In the entire field of education (public or private, higher or lower, parochial or secular) there is no universally accepted method of cost accounting. There have been many
exhaustive investigations of the possibilities of construct-
ing a viable system of educational costing.[6] These have
dealt with factors such as the sizeable differences among
institutions, diverse subjects of instruction, and variations
in faculty needs for time to prepare teaching materials and
to conduct research. These have not been conclusive, nor
have they received wide adoption. Dodds summarizes this
important matter as follows:

Variations in local conditions and academic accounting systems,
not to mention the difficulty of allocating overhead expenses,
make the establishment of valid unit costs in even an institution's business operations a formidable operation, although
obviously less so than in the field of education. The academic
man has good reasons for distrusting the application of unit
costs to teaching and research. Some presidents know from experience how deceptive their influence may be on the judgment of legislatures and governing boards in assessing programs of instruction and research and their right to financial
support. Nevertheless, any college or university is well advised

to record for its own use the comparative costs of its various departments and schools. Although such records of themselves form no valid basis for determining the excellence or worth to our society of a particular program of study or research, they are useful in raising questions, in calling attention to undernourished departments and schools, and in combating extravagance in others.[7]

The monetary problems of colleges and universities which result from below cost pricing (tuition) and lack of access to capital (no financial return to investors) are compounded by this lack of adequate systems of accounts, budgets, operating profiles, projections techniques and general fiscal discipline in most higher institutions. Coombs claims institutional accounting "remains a relatively primitive art" and is adequate for auditing but not for effective management and decision making. Trustees should require, and administrators should develop, techniques in this realm of business and financial reporting that are on a par with those used in industrial organizations and governmental agencies.[8]

Armed with technically correct and intelligently organized financial and statistical reports, trustees and administrators are strategically positioned to recognize weaknesses in their internal operations and to counter external criticisms of their programs.

DOCUMENTATION AND COMMENTARY

[1] Harleigh B. Trecker, *Building the Board,* New York: National Council for Health and Welfare Services, 1960, p. 80.

[2] Morton A. Rauh, *College and University Trusteeship,* Yellow Springs, Ohio: The Antioch Press, 1959, p. 46.

[3] Seymour E. Harris, "College Salaries, Financing of Higher Education and Management of Institutions of Higher Learning," *Bulletin of the American Association of University Professors,* Vol. 44, No. 2, Summer 1958, p. 589

[4] John J. Corson, *Governance of Colleges and Universities,* New York: McGraw-Hill Book Company, 1960, p. 65.

[5] Harold W. Dodds, *The Academic President—Educator or Caretaker,* New York: McGraw-Hill Book Company, 1962, p. 1 and 3.

[6] Such investigations were conducted and have been reported by the Ford Foundation, The Western Conference, New York University and the Associated Colleges of Illinois. In addition to support from philanthropic foundations, several major industrial corporations have indicated intense interest in university cost accounting.

[7] Harold W. Dodds, *op. cit.,* p. 175.

[8] Philip H. Coombs, "*An Economist's Overview.*" Dexter Keezar (ed.) *Financing Higher Education 1960-1970,* New York: McGraw-Hill Book Company, 1959, p. 23.

RESPONSIBILITY FOR PROMOTION AND DEVELOPMENT

Money raising is no longer one man's burden; the president and/or development officer cannot handle it alone; it is a responsibility that must be shared fully by trustees. Neither is it a problem to be solved by one-shot treatment; rather, it is a permanent problem which must be dealt with on a continuous basis. Thus, a development program is an inevitable part of the administrative complex of every college or university—a major part in private institutions and a lesser one in public institutions. It has become a central reason for having trustees.

GENERAL RESPONSIBILITY

Trustees are expected to assume more direct responsibility for and spend more time on public relations and fund raising than any other function. Although the publicly-supported institutions generally are in sounder financial health than the privately-supported institutions, even the former must enlist the active participation of their trustees.

In publicly-supported institutions, fund-raising is accomplished primarily through obtaining increased legislative appropriations. Usually a state university or state board of higher education will encourage its trustees to operate influentially on its behalf with the state legislature. Since trustees of public colleges may not have had previous experience of this kind, it is well for them to be familiar with appropriate procedures.[1]

In privately-supported institutions, fund-raising has become one of the most serious and important problems facing the trustees. All independently-supported institutions are hard pressed. Unless more money is found—and found soon—as Tickton points out, "Many private colleges will decline, will have to merge or will have to close their doors."[2]

Trustees, because of their positions of prominence in the civic, social and economic life of the community, state and nation, are the best qualified members of the institutional "family" to give active leadership in this matter of fund-raising. Given the helpful guidance and support by the president and his staff, raising money for a reputable institution of higher education can be both challenging and satisfying.

There are many professional resources available to assist institutions and their trustees in securing more adequate support for their colleges and universities. There are now well-trained and experienced college administrators who have "majored" in educational promotion and fund-raising; there are many successful fund-raising firms and individual consultants; there are state associations of colleges formed to help with joint appeals; there is the Council for Financial Aid to Education which promotes and publicizes the needs of the schools and colleges to the various sources of support, especially the corporations. These resources are sufficient to enable the trustees and administrators successfully to perform this function, assuming they are properly encouraged and oriented.

FORMULATION OF POLICY

Policy in this area is formulated by the board in response to reports from the president and his chief development officer. In addition, the development committee (or its sub-committees) are involved in actual promotional and developmental work; this work is frequently the pragmatic activity upon which they base their deliberations and, eventually, their policy recommendations to the board.

Because of the importance of using *all possible help* in the external (fund-raising) aspects of the institution's operations, the entire board should evince a close and continuing interest in promotion and development. However, as in the case of other administrative areas in the more complex private institutions, or independent institutions with large boards, there is normally more than one committee, sub-committee or trustee group functioning. The earlier chart suggesting an "organization" for trustees shows the following sub-groups under the promotional committee: development (fund-raising), public relations, government relations (lobbying), planning, and alumni. The smaller institutions will have fewer groups, the larger institutions will have more groups, all institutions will have different groups with varying titles, responsibilities and assignments.

FUND-RAISING PHILOSOPHY

The fund-raising committee or sub-committee is the most important group operating in development affairs. These are the trustees who not only suggest policy in this matter, but actually go out and raise money. Of all the efforts in which a trustee engages as a board member, none is of more vital interest to the institution than this. Only in development are trustees expected to formulate policy and then execute certain aspects of the policy they have formulated.

Collegiate institutions have learned that they must carefully organize their fund-raising program. This is one field where relaxed or slip-shod planning and practice cannot be condoned. The board and the administration must know where the institution is going and how it's going to get there, at least financially. In short, they must be well organized![3]

The chairman and president are ultimately responsible for the organization of the board in this functional area, as in the other major areas. They should be aided by the chief development officer and, possibly, an outside consultant or professional counsel. In terms of organization, trustees need: (1) a clear knowledge of the fund-raising problem and potential of the college or university, (2) an understanding of the channels of communication or relationships within the board and the administration, and (3) an awareness of the methods or techniques of fund-raising.

A development program that wages a continuous and successful campaign for financial support is today an inescapable necessity for any college or university which aims to remain or become strong. Funds adequate to its maintenance and growth must be procured from all potential sources of support.[4] The main problem in higher education today is the same as that faced by Henry Adams a half century ago when he said, "The whole problem of education is one of its cost in money."

FUND-RAISING PRINCIPLES

If trustees are expected to formulate sound policy and otherwise participate actively in the development program of the institution, they should have at least a basic understanding of the elementary principles pertaining to fund-raising. There are three fundamental elements that must exist if success is to be attained in securing voluntary support: First, the prospects or sources of funds; second, the statement of the case or cause; third, the leadership or workers. Fanning the flames of interest in prospects, writing a compelling description of the value of the institution and its goals, and scheduling the actual solicitation, all require professional direction. But, the effective accomplishment of these steps, especially that of solicitation, must include dynamic participation by the trustees.

The first essential is the identification of the *prospective donors* or sources from which the needed funds can be raised. Finding these financial sources, listing them, and evaluating their potential giving ability is an endeavor that should be directed and coordinated by the development officer or an outside professional firm. It is, however, a function in which the trustees have a role. The trustees, being leaders in the social and business community, can assist in pin-pointing persons of wealth, philanthropically inclined business and industrial organizations, charitable foundations and other sources of gifts in the community. In addition, board members can help in the evaluative process of determining how much should be sought from particular sources. Finally, they can suggest the best possible avenues of approach to individuals and companies.

The *case statement* is a written description of the reasons why money is needed, what it will be used for, and the desirable results that will accrue from such use. Usually the case is presented both in person and by publications. The latter can be simple or elaborate, depending upon the circumstances. They are customarily prepared by the public relations or development office of the institution.

The third principle is the *leadership*, the workers or the manpower to be involved in fund-raising. The president and the other members of the academic community can help in making calls on certain prospective donors. But, experience has proven that the greatest success in fund-raising comes from the use of an intermediary—a friendly third party between the institutional officer and the prospective donor—and there are no better intermediaries than dedicated, informed, articulate board members. However, scheduling contacts and coordinating the over-all effort remains the responsibility of the development office.

In discussing personnel involved in the pursuit of money, it is well to note the three kinds of people concerned. There are (1) the *volunteers* (trustees, alumni and friends of the institution), (2) the *paid staff* (regular employees of the institution), and (3) the *professional aides* (outsiders temporarily employed by the institution). Because large scale campaigns require the participation of thousands of men and women (one recent fund-raising campaign had more than 5,000 solicitors spread from Maine to California) it is necessary to add to the regular development staff outside professional help. A well-conceived campaign or long-range program will bring into action all possible trustee and other voluntary leadership, because a "staff-oriented" operation is usually weak and outside professional fund-raisers do not normally solicit gifts. On the latter point, a frequent error is that once a professional fund-raising firm is engaged, the institutional staff and lay leaders can relax, heave a sigh of relief, and provide only nominal effort.[5]

In advancing the cause of the college or university, all members of the governing board (not merely its development committee) should volunteer their services. While not all may wish to make solicitations and actually ask for money, there are so many tasks in this domain of fund-raising that ample opportunity exists for the utilization of a variety of skills, experiences, and temperaments.

In order to properly employ the three elements mentioned above (prospects, case, leadership), trustees must understand some of the other principles related to effective fund-raising. Entire books have been written on these points; what follows herein is merely a brief summary: The institution must have a sound educational program because that is why donors contribute. Since the college or university performs a unique service for society, it merits the support of society and has every right to expect such support. Fund-raising, as a science, should be directed by a full-time expert; fund-raising as an art, should be influenced by lay leaders. This function is not impossible to learn, nor beneath the dignity of any trustee. All possible avenues of support should be exploited regularly and thoroughly; this encompasses the entire spectrum from the annual giving of unrestricted funds to the intensive campaign at periodic intervals for capital gifts.

PRIVATE VERSUS PUBLIC SUPPORT

The dual system of public *and* private higher education has helped make this the best educated nation the world has ever known. This dual system should be continued. Assuming the acceptance of this contention—that America needs both public and private institutions of higher education—it then follows that some thought should be given to their support. The public colleges and universities traditionally have been financed by tax sources; the private institutions by tuitions, endowment income, gifts and grants.

This traditional division of support is undergoing revolutionary change. Tax-supported institutions are now actively competing with the independently-supported institutions for funds from the private sectors (*i.e.*, wealthy individuals and corporations). Partly because of this competition, the private colleges have had to turn to the federal government for financial assistance. There are many thoughtful leaders in higher education and in other walks of life, who deplore this change in the methods of support because they feel it will change to some extent the basic character of the institutions themselves.

If these amounts should be enormously increased, the concern expressed for the continuance of the difference between public and private higher education might be justified. Enormous increases in the amount of support could conceivably come about if the public institutions expand their already active fund-raising programs with private contributors. Such action might push the independent colleges to the point where they felt it necessary to turn to the state or federal government for corresponding financial aid.

In dealing directly with nearly two hundred of the largest corporations in the nation for the past fifteen years, it has become apparent to me that each has certain prescribed limits to the amount it can contribute to higher education. Experience in dealing with foundations and individual philanthropists over the same period indicates that they, too, are not possessed of unlimited resources.

The argument advanced against this simple example of financial logic is that if a state university it doing a good promotional job, this will help the private institutions. This is true to the extent that the public institution is merely "promoting"; but if it is also "collecting" (and who promotes without expecting to collect?) then it must follow that since no source of funds yet discovered is unlimited, dollars donated to one institution cannot be donated to another.

In summary, the point should be made that all of higher education needs and deserves greater support. The dual system of both public and private institutions should be continued and strengthened. A certain amount of blending of financial support and character of operation, presents no serious problem. But avoidance of massive changes in either financial support or academic character is imperative. Massive changes can be avoided if we encourage public institutions to secure greater support from their respective legislatures and encourage the private institutions to secure greater support from voluntary sources.[6]

PUBLIC RELATIONS PHILOSOPHY

Trustees are in a commanding position to interpret the institution's program to the public—and to interpret public sentiment to the institution. This interpretation is in the broad sense considered an integral part of public relations and a natural function for board members. Trustees should help bridge the gap between "town and gown". There are several ways in which a board member can serve as intermediary:

(a) By interesting qualified high school graduates in his college and in discouraging unqualified students from applying.
(b) By remaining in touch with alumni in his area in order to communicate information to and from the college.
(c) By introducing faculty and staff members to groups and individuals in his community in order to provide a dissemination of knowledge and broaden the sphere of interest of the college.
(d) By representing the college with the major media of communication in his area to improve the image of his college and keep it before the public.
(e) By helping to place recent graduates in positions for which they are qualified and in which they might be interested.

The public relations philosophy gaining greatest acceptance in most colleges and universities is that of providing all possible information to all interested parties. Another way of stating this open door policy is to say that the higher institutions realize that the days of the ivory tower are gone and that the public has much to offer the college or university. This includes not only moral and financial support, but also scientific, cultural and social assistance with its educational programs. Of course, the selfish reason for having a strong public relations program is to win friends and influence people, thus, ultimately, to advance the cause of the institution.

Like fund-raising, public relations is both a science and an art. As such, it requires professional direction. While the president is normally the key person in any P.R. program, the public relations officer should be at his elbow assisting and encouraging him in this work. The same officer should be available to maximize the efforts of board members engaged in public relations projects.

PUBLIC RELATIONS PRINCIPLES

The underlying principle of public relations is to tell your story as honestly and effectively as possible. It is obvious that a good public relations officer will endeavor to have his press release or his brochure, his president or his trustees, accentuate the positive and improve the image of the institution. A second principle is that a sound program of public relations is more than publicity or the dissemination of information; it must also reflect community attitudes back to the institution; it is, indeed, a two-way street. This means that the institution is better able to serve its public and be a part of that public (rather than apart from it).

Another principle of college public relations is that of disseminating appropriate information and, thus, building up the image of the institution so that academically qualified and otherwise desirable high school students will wish to apply for admission. Effective public relations programs emphasize those features of the institution that are different from competitors. In addition, they usually imply that an excellent general education and an interestingly balanced program of extra-curricular activities are offered.

Many media of communications are used in telling the story. In the early days, the case for the institution was stated in person by the president. Later refinements included all kinds and varieties of printed material delivered in person (by representatives of the college) and by direct mail. Currently, institutions of higher education are re-

cratic personnel involved. These people are sometimes not radio, television, and paid newspaper advertising.

The responsibility of the public relations office extends beyond the routine operations of outward communication through press releases, advertising, the publishing of reports and catalogues, the making of speeches, and so on. It embraces in addition, a cycle of communication between the college or university and its various publics, in which the institution *listens* as well as talks. P.R. is a systematic process grounded upon a studied understanding of the role of the enterprise in society in the broadest sense, a process designed to include as active participants all the more important groups, such as trustees, associated with the institution.[7]

GOVERNMENT RELATIONS

Publicly-supported institutions have, traditionally, had to maintain good relationships, normally through their boards, with the appropriating authority. With the increase in federal aid to privately-supported colleges and universities, even these traditionally independent institutions are seeking to strengthen their rapport with government agencies.

Lobbying has always been a bad word in educational and cultural circles. To a lesser extent, "public relations" and "fund-raising" have also had questionable connotations. Actually, all three activities are related, are essential to the advancement of worthy educational causes, and are activities in which members of boards of trustees should be involved.

These related functions are perhaps more essential in dealing with government, than with the general public, because of the stigma attached to the political or bureau-cratic personnel involved. These people are sometimes not college-educated, are removed from the college campus, and are unfamiliar with the pressing problems of the higher institutions. Consequently, they need some pressures on them; they need a lobby or at least a representative of the institution who can give them the information, inspiration, and assurances they must have if they are to vote adequate funds for the institution. Although some states' boards of regents employ professional lobbyists, in most instances the president (or chancellor) and the board chairman (or other trustees) carry this responsibility.[8]

PLANNING FOR TOMORROW

One of the most serious oversights in higher education has been the lack of adequate planning for the future. Until there is such planning, and until it is translated into a "blueprint for tomorrow", even the best development programs are severely limited. Sound, long-range planning involves establishing the objectives of the college or university, and its needs for staff, facilities and funds to achieve these objectives in the future. Once made, long-term plans should be reviewed and revised; the blueprint should, like the budget, be considered a *flexible* guide. This kind of planning requires the application of scientific and objective methods and techniques in place of subjective judgments. Every college and university should have an office of planning (possibly integrated with institutional research) that provides staff leadership to the board and the president in these affairs. Indeed, some institutions have formed trustees' committees, sub-committees or *ad hoc* groups to ponder and deliberate upon the direction in which the college or university should travel, how it should get there, and when it should arrive at particular points.[9]

One of the functions of a planning office should be the establishment and charting of institutional responsibility and authority. The organization chart may never tell the whole story of channels of communication and specific relationships, but such a systematic, graphic description of lines, titles and boxes does help to clarify certain connections.

Although the promotional or developmental area is not the only one with which a planning office would involve itself, because of the number of activities and general complexity of this area, a descriptive chart is offered at this point to illustrate one of the operations of a planning office and to propose a form of organization for this administrative division called "promotion." This chart is based upon a more detailed and complicated version originally prepared by the Council for Financial Aid to Education, Inc.

OTHER PROMOTIONAL FACETS

Every college or university has its own organizational problems in promotion. For that reason, each has its own special approach to solving these. However, there are some common threads running through the fabric of each. One of the most important and related to all colleges and universities is the use of the trustee. Since members of governing boards are giving so generously of their time and talent to developmental projects, it is logical that they should be kept fully informed of all aspects of this function. By knowing what's happening in the field and how other institutions solve problems, board members are in a better position to solve the problems of their own institutions.

**PROPOSED ORGANIZATION CHART FOR A
LARGE UNIVERSITY'S PROMOTIONAL DIVISION**

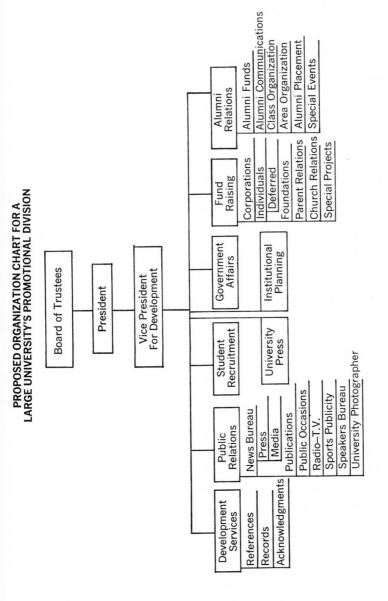

In addition to the major promotional functions, a brief description of some minor promotional functions is appropriate at this point.

Within this area there should be a person or office handling each aspect of *development services* as indicated on the chart. Adequate and accurate records are essential to the success of all efforts in fund-raising.

Under the general banner of *public relations* come such operations as the news bureau (including the press and other information media), publications, public occasions, radio and television (as educational media), sports publicity, speakers bureau, and the university photographer.

Many institutions relate their programs of student *recruitment* to the promotional efforts. This function includes attracting students, but excludes admissions efforts (as these are part of the academic or administrative area).

Fund-Raising includes such sub-divisions as corporations, individuals, deferred giving, foundations, parents, special projects and (in denominationally-related institutions) church relations. There are other phases of support programs which could be included, but they would be the exception (rather than the rule) in most institutions.

The *University Press* is a function that might be related to the academic or administrative area of operations, but the current trend is to have it close by the promotional, public relations and publications functions.

Alumni Relations is one of the most important development functions of any institution. It is promotional in character and is, therefore, listed in this division. Among the facets of this office are the alumni fund, alumni communications, class organization, area organization, alumni placement and special alumni events.

Government Affairs and *Planning* are relatively new areas under promotion. They have been presented in separate sections earlier in this chapter.

DOCUMENTATION AND COMMENTARY

[1] T. R. McConnell, *A General Pattern for American Public Higher Education*, New York: McGraw-Hill Company, 1962, p. 190.

[2] Sidney Tickton, as reported in the *New York Times*, September 25, 1961.

[3] John A. Pollard, *Fund-Raising For Higher Education*, New York: Harper and Row, 1958, p. 250.

[4] Frank Sparks, *Financing for the Future*, New York: Council for Financial Aid to Education, 1960, p. 7.

[5] Robert F. Duncan, *Strategy in the Raising of Money*, New York: Kersting, Brown and Company, 1962, p. 12.

[6] Gordon N. Ray, "*Conflict and Cooperation in American Higher Education.*" Dexter M. Keezer, Editor, *Financing Higher Education 1960-70*, New York: McGraw-Hill Company, 1959, p. 106.

[7] Richard Eells, *Corporation Giving in a Free Society*, New York: Harper and Row, 1956, p. 171.

[8] For an objective and detailed analysis of the role of government in higher education attention is invited to Algo D. Henderson, *Policies and Practices in Higher Education*, New York: Harper and Row, 1960, Chapter 17.

[9] Arnold F. Emch, "*Long Range Planning for Colleges and Universities*", a monograph published by Booze, Allen and Hamilton, Chicago, Ill., p. 15.

10 ADDITIONAL RESPONSIBILITIES OF THE BOARD

Some of the board's activities fall outside the academic, financial and promotional divisions, and relate to such matters as presidential selection, trustee recruiting, orientation and training. In addition to these specific activities, there are other important considerations that are not easily classified and usually involve the full board, rather than a particular committee.

LEGAL ASPECTS OF BOARD MEMBERSHIP

The governing board is the legally constituted "corpus" or body in each institution. With respect to the legal aspects of the trusteeship, Chambers has remarked that, "The governing board is almost always a corporation—an artificial person having a legal entity. In the eyes of the law, this ghostly legal entity *is* necessary."[1] As such, the board has a

clear responsibility to the state through the chartering and/
or incorporating agency. Generally, colleges and universities are chartered by the department of education in the
state where they operate. Thus, that department has a
loosely supervisory relationship to the board in which it has
vested sweeping powers and broad authority. It is seldom,
however, that trustees come in contact with officials of the
state department of education, since these people work
closely with the presidents and other administrative officers
of the various institutions.

Since the board has final, legal authority over the college
or university, it is the high court of appeals or "last resort."
As such, it is responsible for everything that takes place at
the institution. Although the president is the chief executive, his power is derived from the board. While the board
is not an executive body and does not make operational decisions, it can reverse a president, if necessary, by removing
him.

Some boards review all major presidential (or administrative) decisions. Some boards (or their grievance committees) hear complaints from faculty, students or other persons who feel an unfair administrative decision (or interpretation of policy) has been made against them. Not every
board action will be unanimous in always backing presidential recommendations; but, if there are many rejections of
the proposals or decisions of the president, he should ask
for a vote of confidence. If it is negative, he should resign.
By the same token, the board can, at times, serve as a protective shield for the president and the institution by reply-
ing to unjust attacks as a unified group in a statement of
policy. The protective role of the board is vitally important
to the freedom of the institution.

In summary, and according to the Paley report from Columbia, the major legal responsibilities that devolve upon the trustees are:"(1) To select and appoint the president of the university; (2) To be finally responsible for the acquisition, conservation, and management of the university's funds and properties; (3) To oversee and approve the kind of education offered by the university, and make certain that its quality meets the highest standards possible."[2]

MORAL ASPECTS OF BOARD MEMBERSHIP

In addition to their weighty legal responsibility in governing their colleges and universities, trustees must assume a heavy moral responsibility. This entails an understanding of and appreciation for the work of the institution. It means that the trustee must learn to feel deeply his relationship and see clearly his opportunity for advising and assisting in furthering the cause. It does not mean that the trustee relinquishes his objectivity, but, rather, he tempers it with the acceptance of the fact that he is part of an intellectual, spiritual and emotional enterprise—one of the great cultural determinants of our society—and he acts accordingly.

He must understand the role or function of the higher institution. Most educators would summarize that role or function in five parts: It is a

1. Repository of knowledge (through its library, museum, professors, etc.).
2. Discoverer of new knowledge (through its research, experimentation, codification, etc.).
3. Dispenser of knowledge (through its teaching, counseling, guiding, etc.).
4. Provider of community service (through its clinics, conferences, area studies, etc.).

5.   Promoter of world understanding (through the above four
     functions, plus its exchange of students and faculty with
     foreign institutions).

Armed with an understanding of the function of higher
education generally and his institution particularly, the
trustee can better comprehend what is expected of him in
governing sympathetically, wisely and justly. He can fulfill
the moral responsibilities of his board membership best
when he is completely informed.

SELECTION OF THE PRESIDENT

There are those who claim, with some justification, that
the most critical function of the board of trustees is the selection and election of the president. As such, this process
deserves thoughtful consideration on the part of every trustee. The influence of the president upon his institution, and
the cumulative influence of all higher institutions on our
way of life, makes imperative the selection of only the finest
kind of college or university president.[3]

There are several simple, yet essential steps that the trustees should take in logical sequence in securing a president.
If the board is a large one, a presidential search committee
should be formed. This committee should secure from the
board, the administration, and the faculty, a general consensus of the kind of president desired. It should contact
all the sources where possible nominations might be secured. This includes the institution itself, other similar institutions, the learned societies and the professional associations. In addition, many committees turn to the great foundations, to government agencies (such as the U. S. Office of
Education) and the federations of colleges (such as the

American Council on Education, the Association of American Colleges, and the Independent College Funds of America).

Armed with a long list of possible candidates, the committee should perform a careful screening job. When the list has been narrowed down to eight or ten names, these people should be asked if they are *interested* and if they would be *willing* to serve if elected. This may reduce the list down to five or six leading candidates all of whom should be interviewed by the committee. Although the committee should make the final proposal of two or three candidates to the full board, the administration and faculty should have an opportunity at least informally, to meet the candidates and share reactions with the committee.

There are many check lists that have been devised to aid in the selection of college and university presidents. Any such list will help trustees in the evaluative process if they bear in mind certain fundamentals. First, the candidate must have a sound education, preferably culminating in one or more earned doctor's degrees. Second, the candidate should have had some training in a scholarly discipline, in pedagogy, and in administration. Third, the candidate should have had some experience as a faculty member and an administrator, hopefully in higher education. Fourth, the candidate should have done some travel, research, and writing at different sites and possibly abroad. Fifth, the candidate should have a pleasing appearance, temperament and personality; and be vigorous and in sound health. Sixth, the candidate should have a well-rounded grasp of the world situation, education generally and higher education specifically; he should know his way around in intellectual and cultural circles. Seventh, he should have the leadership skills of being able to address, influence and secure action from both large and small groups. Eighth, he should be a man of personal integrity, moral strength, good will and optimistic outlook. Ninth, he should be a "man of management" as well as a "man of learning". Tenth, he should want the job![4]

Obviously, it is not easy to locate people with all these fundamental qualifications—but they do exist and it is the job of the trustees to find them. Once they have been identified, screened, and interviewed, one should be promptly elected. A serious problem in American higher education is the proclivity on the part of many boards to drag out the selection and election of a new president. This is most unfortunate because, unlike an industrial or military organization, educational institutions seldom have an executive vice president (or deputy commander) ready, willing and able to assume the presidency. Thus, many colleges and universities have struggled on for long periods with acting or interim presidents who were loathe to provide the strong leadership so greatly needed.

RELATIONSHIPS WITH THE PRESIDENT

A fundamental facet of organizational procedure in terms of the relationship between the president and the board should be that of a chief executive officer operating within the framework of policies established by the trustees as a group. There is a thin, but discernible line of demarcation between *governance* (the board's function) and *administration* (the president's function).

The president should be a full member of the board, but need not have voting privilege. The president should encourage the chairman to serve as presiding officer, but should assist him in running the meetings. Although the chairman should speak for the board, only the president should speak for the institution. The president's rapport with the trustees, especially with the chairman, should be warm and friendly. Together the president and the chairman (and to a lesser extent the other trustees and senior administrators) constitute the leadership team. Board members and staff members each have specific responsibilities, as well as common or shared responsibilities. The role of the administration is to organize and provide the faculty and facilities for the educational program; the role of the board is to determine and provide the conditions and policies under which the staff may operate its program.[5]

Newer concepts of governance and administration suggest that there are some areas of joint concern on the part of the board and the administration. Policy development has increasingly become a common endeavor. Sorenson has said that, "Policy *formulation* and planning are the responsibility of both board and committee members and of the professional staff . . . policy *determination* is the responsibility of the board alone."[6]

Trustees and administrators have much to learn from each other. Because he meets with, and coordinates the affairs of, both the faculty and the board, the president is the central person on campus. He can be, and usually is, instrumental and influential in directing the activities of both bodies, even though he may not preside over their meetings.

TENURE CONSIDERATIONS

One of the major differences between industry and education is that the latter takes on some employes "for life." That is, colleges and universities in contracting with certain classes of professors traditionally have extended them indefinite tenure. This means that the institution accepts the obligation of employing these people until they wish to leave or until they reach retirement age. This is a serious responsibility and requires careful financial planning. Consequently, when faculty members are eligible for promotion or entitled to tenure, such appointments are usually made (or at least ratified) by the full board.

Generally administrators serve indefinitely, but on a year-to-year basis. Occasionally a three to five-year contract is offered by the board to outstanding administrators.[7] Nonacademic personnel, other than officers of the institution, are not usually provided with any contractual arrangement.

Board members of public institutions normally serve for a period of three to five years, although some terms last as long as fifteen years. Board members of private institutions frequently serve up to the mandatory retirement age, because these boards are usually self-perpetuating and trustees are invariably re-elected. The mandatory retirement age varies from 60 to 80; a few institutions have no mandatory retirement age. Because of the tendency of people to become more conservative with advancing years, it would seem desirable to seek younger trustees, have a definite term or tenure (*i.e.*, five years), allow for re-election, but have a specific mandatory retirement age.

Having a specific term or period on the board and being automatically rotated off appears to be a salutary new trend even in private institutions. The advantages of limited tenure can be summarized as follows: First, rotation provides a systematic way of bringing new people (with their new ideas, perspectives and skills) on to the board. Second, rotation, by enlisting new trustees, broadens the base of community interest, understanding and support. Third, rotation keeps the leadership from becoming ingrown, possessive and self-perpetuating. Fourth, rotation provides a painless method of separating non-productive members from the board. Fifth, rotation tends to attract busy, competent people who will accept such responsibility for only a specified, limited period of time.[8]

REPORTS TO THE BOARD

As implied earlier, much of the business of the board is conducted by oral reports at meetings and written reports circulated periodically. Because so much of its work is based upon reports, a board of trustees has every right to expect such reports, regardless of who presents them, to be as *concise* as possible, and yet as *comprehensive* as necessary. Reports vary from those that are frequent, brief, informal, and limited in distribution, to those that are infrequent, long, formal, and disseminated in large numbers for the edification of the public. The president's annual report is a classic illustration of the latter.

Reports reach the board from many sources. Among the usual groups are the various trustee committees or subcommittees; among the individuals are the chairman, president, and senior administrative officers. Many experienced trustees feel that all committee reports should be channelled through the chairman or president so that one of these key figures will be familiar with what is coming up and can plan for it on the agenda. Certainly all reports from administrative officers should clear through the president.

Management consultants stress the importance of the causal relationship between a board's efficiency and the president's effectiveness in communicating with it.[9] These consultants have been properly critical of the skills of presidents in this department. In addition to proper methods of communicating, the wise president, possibly with the guidance of his chairman, will avoid bringing to the board reports that present small or insignificant details for consideration.[10]

DOCUMENTATION AND COMMENTARY

[1] Merritt M. Chambers, "Who is the University", *Journal of Higher Education,* June 1959, p. 321.

[2] William S. Paley, "The Role of the Trustees of Columbia University", New York: Columbia University, November 4, 1957, p. 20.

[3] Harold W. Dodds, *The Academic President—Educator or Caretaker,* New York: McGraw-Hill Company, 1962, p. 261.

[4] Myron F. Wicker, *Handbook for Trustees,* Nashville, Tenn.: The Methodist Church, 1957, p. 17.

[5] Harleigh B. Trecker, *Building the Board,* New York: National Publicity Council for Health and Welfare Services, 1960, p. 15.

[6] Roy Sorenson, *The Art of Board Membership,* New York: Association Press, 1950, p. 23.

[7] Football coaches, development officers and presidents (in that order of frequency) are the only staff members this writer has known to receive more lengthy contracts than the regular one-year option.

[8] Trecker, *op. cit.,* p. 34.

[9] Dodds, *op. cit.,* p. 249.

[10] Gerald P. Burns, "How Consultants Can Help Solve Problems of Higher Education", *College and University Business,* Vol. 37, No. 3, September, 1964.

<table>
<tr><td>11</td><td>

THE FUTURE OF THE TRUSTEESHIP
</td></tr>
</table>

This chapter treats of discernible trends which might affect the future role of the trustees. In the light of these trends, some suggested ways and means are offered by which the role of the board can be clarified for the individual trustees and made more meaningful for their institutions.

THE ORIENTED TRUSTEE

Duncan says, "There are 22,000 college trustees in America. Is it not true that much of our country's future is in their hands?"[1] Dodds indicates there are 30,000 board members and that they are vitally important to education and the nation.[2] Nearly all of the trustees and regents with whom I have discussed these points favor an affirmative answer to Duncan's question and complete agreement with Dodds' statement.

As detailed earlier, trustees should welcome (and administrators should provide) adequate orientation for the new board member and "continuing education" for the experienced or long-time board member. Colleges and universities are complex institutions whose intricacies should be explained to the trustees. These board members can render better service and can be of far greater value if they are advised and kept informed of the institution's program, problems and potentialities.

There are those who feel that trustee education, training and orientation is a personal problem that should be solved by the board member himself. But it is unreasonable to assume that such self-education will be enough. There must be continuing learning experiences offered by qualified professionals if the board member is to remain abreast of new departures in his institution and new dimensions in higher education.[3]

THE ACTIVE TRUSTEE

A well-oriented and fully-informed trustee is prepared to become a helpful and active trustee. The admonition that trustees should be "worked" is an opinion shared by many leaders in the college field. It would be a waste of time, money and effort if, after trustees were selected, recruited and oriented, their time and talents were not utilized to the maximum. While no authorities advocate a full-time job for trustees, key trustees interviewed said that giving a considerable amount of time to the board was essential.

The "working" or using of trustees to the fullest requires the practice of tact and judgment. While their best efforts must continuously be called forth, if overworked, they may react unfavorably. Thus, their talents must be carefully assessed by the administration and their interests made known to the chairman and president. It is clear that the most active board members are the most valuable board members. Of course, their activity must be properly directed by the chairman toward governance rather than administration.

College government covers a broad field. Occasionally, trustees are overwhelmed by its nature and scope, especially on the academic side. But, it is apparent that the trend of the future is for more, rather than less, activity on the part of the trustees with greater attention being paid to the educational program of the institution. Trustees need exposure to all facets of the institution's program. This includes the *academic* as the most important activity on campus. Involvement begets interest and understanding.

THE STRONG PRESIDENT

An individual executive, not a committee or a board, is the most efficient instrument for final decision-making. There are inevitable irrelevancies, compromises and log-rolling activities that block or delay decisions and action in committee and board meetings. Boards of trustees, alumni committees, faculty senates and other bodies have at various times operated educational institutions. Although these efforts proved successful in Europe, Andrews' comments on the American system are interesting. "No institution of learning has tried the plan of assigning its main executive function to a faculty or to a faculty committee without complete or relative failure. On the other hand—a significant fact—American higher education dates its present era of triumph exactly from the time when colleges began centralizing executive power and, so to speak, 'mobilizing' their presidents. . . . It lies mainly with the president to shape a university's task, ideals, standards, policies, ambitions, to determine what it shall be or try to be."[4] This kind of executive leadership does not infringe upon the policy leadership of the board.

Some students of higher education recommend that the chairmanship, like the presidency, should be occupied by a paid professional. Along this line, Cattell recommended that the office of the president should be divided and filled by two men of different type. One would be an educational expert in charge of the internal administration; the other a man of prominence in the community to be in charge of external affairs.[5] A study of this device indicates that, although proposed by Cattell in 1902, it has had some current experimentation. Despite the fact that several large urban universities tried variations of this theme with a chancellor-president team, it has not achieved broad usage.[6]

An analysis of the various plans discloses that the modification in the presidency (designed to divide the position and its functions between two executives) operated in similar fashion in at least four institutions. The development took on the appearance of a senior partner or elder statesman operating in association with a junior partner or assistant. Because of this apparent schism in authority, the assumption of responsibility was not equally shared. This dual approach to the presidency (where the two executives are virtually co-equal) did not gain wide acceptance because it violated a cardinal principle of administration—that authority must be commensurate with responsibility and some *one* person must assume ultimate responsibility for the executive leadership of the college or university.

The purpose of this brief treatment of the presidency is to

shed light on the relationships which he has with his board. Along this line, it is interesting to note what some elder statesmen have said of these relationships. Hill suggests that "The position of the president ... remains important but anomalous, autocratic but often legally impotent, vaguely defined, yet conspicuous."[7] I concur with this view, but suggest that trustees have an important role to play in reducing the autocratic elements by strengthening the moral authority of the president. Horrigan says, "The duties of the average American college president have become complex and even a little harrowing... The average president survives in office for only about five or six years. This mortality rate may be sufficiently high to prompt the labor statisticians to look thoughtful and to ask some pointed questions ..."[8] Selden's research study reported in *Liberal Education* of March, 1960, indicates with statistical accuracy that the average length of service of the current presidents in office at all types of colleges and universities is 8.1 years. Rainey believes ". . . that the fundamental difficulty with the office of university president arises out of the current system of controlling modern universities ... He has vast responsibilities for all phases of the life and welfare of the university, but he has no power. Under the present system of university control and administration, a university presidency is a hazardous and often frustrating experience. It offers little or no security, very little of opportunity for educational statesmanship, and, perhaps, most important of all, little opportunity for self-realization."[9] I concur and, in the light of the earlier personal research, evaluate Rainey's conclusions as being factual, although depressing and pessimistic.

Based upon views such as these, plus the judgments

of other experienced trustees, it appears that the American college presidency needs strengthening. The trustees constitute one group that can and should provide such strengthening.

Although the board itself offers little promise as an agency for the design and administration of the curriculum, since the trustees have the final authority and accountability, they must find, adapt, invent or create a new and suitable instrument through which the curriculum and methods of instruction may better contribute to the cause of liberal education.

There is a trend developing for boards to expect their presidents to exert a restraining influence on the proliferation of the curriculum and provide positive, creative educational leadership in suggesting new, progressive academic departures. This trend is developing because the president is the only person to whom both boards and faculties can turn for this kind of leadership.

THE EFFECTIVE FACULTY

With interaction between faculty and trustees so infrequent, one group knows little about the other. Traditionally, the president had bridged the gap. It now appears that, to serve the best interests of all members of the institutional family and the welfare of the institution itself, it would be desirable if there were closer rapport between the faculty and trustees.

Because there is a widespread stereotype of the trustee being a "man of action" and the professor a "man of thought", there are some unreasonable suspicions between the two groups. It is possible that these are being dispelled, at least in part, by the growing practice of having faculty members from other institutions serving as board members.

An effective faculty is one that has a challenging role to play, is well qualified to play it, and plays it with satisfaction. There has been little satisfaction, for the last several decades, with faculty salaries being so deplorably low. This situation certainly had an adverse effect on the morale and enthusiasm of teachers. Despite the very serious financial plight of the liberal college, there is little genuine appreciation among individual members of the faculty of the urgency of the problem. The deterioration of the economic status of the teaching profession has been gradual and is not obvious in any one generation. Educational and public leadership must now convey to the college teacher the fact that there is a deep national interest in reversing the process of professional deterioration. The trustees, rather than the faculty itself, the administration, the students, or any other group, must take the leadership in improving faculty salaries, and, thus making the professional life more satisfying.

Some researchers, like Harris, blame the faculty for this unhappy situation. "Faculty pay would be much higher if faculties were more disposed to economize without seriously affecting the educational product. What can be accomplished is suggested by President Hutchins' experience in the Great Depression at Chicago. The faculty dropped 450 courses when the President announced that the one objective was to maintain faculty pay. This the faculty achieved by a drastic reduction in the college offering."[10]

In an attempt to make faculty life more stimulating, many boards are striving to obtain better communication with the teaching staff. Several presidents admit spending too much time on things like fund-raising and too little time with their faculties.

Corson summarizes the situation by saying:

Most presidents the author has encountered lament their in-ability to spend more time with their faculties. In most institutions there is little, if any direct contact between trustees and the faculty. Four factors underlie the apparent lack of communication among faculties and president and trustees. First and most important is the infinitely greater specialization among members of the university staff than is found in industry or government. Second, the individuality of thought typical of faculty members poses special problems for communication. Third, the hierarchy of deans and department heads in many institutions cannot be directed to communicate and interpret to the faculty as the foremen and division heads in business can be ordered to pass the word along. Fourth, confusion generally prevails about what matters should be communicated to all the faculty, *e.g.*, Is it useful or wasteful to inform the professor of history on the cost of a new furnace, and should he be asked to offer an opinion on whether a new furnace shall be installed?[11]

The faculty should have considerable responsibility and authority for the design of the curriculum. Moreover, as more faculty members are elected to boards and as trustees from all walks of life receive better orientation, board members generally become knowledgeable about and concerned with the academic program. The trend in this area affecting the trustees' role is that of their desiring to work more closely with the administration, faculty and students in curricular matters insofar as policy is concerned.

In selecting an instrument or mechanism for the purpose of reconstructing the curriculum, the trustees should realize that the change-over will take many years of careful work, and that flexibility and adaptability to experience, to circumstance and to the unpredictable, are essential to avoid rigidity and the inevitable friction that responds to a stubborn and arrogant force. If the instrument (possibly the presidency) must be sensitive and flexible, so too must be the approach of the trustees toward its operation and development.

Many thoughtful professors with whom this matter was discussed agreed that academic administration is not only necessary, but also that in every complex college or university, efficient administration is and must be the cornerstone of effective educational operation. Ever since 1900, some faculty members have been seeking greater power, not alone on academic affairs, but on finance, administration and major policy issues. At a few institutions, such as Reed (1911) and Oberlin (1925) their requests were granted. After World War I, several writers raised the question of abolishing trustees and presidents. The agitation waned because it lacked support of the general public and the alumni, and because the trustees and presidents yielded some of their prerogatives to the faculties.[12]

It has been suggested over the years that students should play a more important role in the governance and administration of their respective colleges and universities. Since its founding in 1911, Reed College has encouraged the participation of students in all college affairs even to the point of meeting informally with the trustees. In various institutions at different times in the past half-century, students virtually seized the leadership and took specific action on such matters as forcing general university reorganization (University of California at Berkeley), ousting the president (University of New Mexico) and establishing curriculum reform (Harvard University). While there is little rationale for these actions, some student participation in governance might prove desirable. Beck strongly advocates student representation on boards of trustees at least to the extent of giving students a minority voice in governance.[13]

THE EDUCATED STUDENT

Everything that the trustee does (or fails to do) has some relationship to the education of students in his institution. Granted that the trustees seldom see their students, nevertheless board action always affects the persons who compose the college or university.

In a college or university, decisions on curriculum, faculty selection and promotion, admissions, budgets and even buildings, must, in the final analysis, be based upon judgment about what will contribute most to the education of the students. The essential activity in higher education takes place in the minds of these students and their professors—the ideas produced by the scholar's intellect and their communication to the minds of students. This emphasizes that the student body is the primary reason for the existence of the institution, and that trustees should take cognizance of this fact.

The aim of every board should be to develop the overall policies of its institution in such a way that the finest kind of educational program commensurate with institutional limitations (*i.e.*, finances, personnel, philosophy) is offered to the students. Since their decisions directly affect the students, able and interested board members make an effort to know the students. Knowledge of the student body can be secured from the reports of the president, other administrators, and faculty members; but, for first-hand impressions, at least some of it should come from direct (even though informal and occasional) contact with the students.

The president, and possibly the deans, have the heavy responsibility of reporting student affairs honestly, accurately, and frequently to the trustees. The president should secure and maintain good rapport with, and retain the confidence of, the student body as well as other groups on campus. Cowley expands on this point by saying, "Above all else a college president, it seems to me, must be a leader. He must lead his students, his faculty, and his board ... He and his associates must follow three democratic principles of administration: (1) the board of trustees must be democratic and not dictatorial, (2) the faculty must have freedom of speech on academic policies, and (3) the students must have practice in the democratic management of their own affairs."[14]

THE FUNCTIONAL BOARD

When asked how the board membership is changing, trustees and presidents are nearly unanimous in their response that the job is evolving from an honorific to a functional assignment. Assuming the trustees are capable, dedicated men and women, more purposeful activity on behalf of their institutions proves welcome.

As higher education faces a future of automation in pedagogy, enormous enrollments, explosions of knowledge, faculty shortages, student demonstrations, and other traumatic challenges, it is abundantly clear that new dimensions of leadership are needed. Since these difficulties are frequently related to finances, and since the board has the major responsibility for proper financing of the institution, it seems that the trustees may be the one campus group that can solve these problems.

To be most effective in meeting these challenges, the board should be carefully selected, properly oriented and kept fully informed about and active in the total affairs of the institution. Indeed, there are those who hold that board members have a broader responsibility than merely working for their own college. Patrick has observed that we must be ". . . concerned with the dynamics of economic and social development, and we must employ the proper tools and methods. All of us must speak and act forcefully and intelligently for all higher education, not just for our own institution, our own association, or our own pet method of support."[15] While not all trustees are competent to speak for higher education, they should be knowledgeable about a broader segment than a single institution.

There is a metamorphosis occurring in higher education itself that affects the trusteeship. This is the change in balance in our dual system of public and private higher education. In 1950 private institutions enrolled approximately one-half of all college students. In 1965 they enrolled only about one-third, and this trend is continuing! Lloyd's comment on this enrollment shift is, "A second change in the position of private colleges and universities occurred with the appearance of the great state universities, with large budgets from tax funds, low tuition, and entrance requirements quite different from those of private institutions. They face still further large increases in enrollment during the next decade, when the number of students seeking admission to colleges is expected to double. Private institutions must come to grips with new policies about enrollments and with the educational and other consequences of sudden change in size and in pressures under which they must operate."[16] The road ahead for the private institution is bound to be a rough one. He suggests that this new position of private universities—flanked on one side by large and rapidly expanding tax-supported, low-tuition institutions, and on the other by huge and rapidly growing government and industrial training departments and laboratories—has not only given them new potentialities, but new problems as well. This change in balance is a serious problem that may threaten the very survival of the dual system of public and private higher education. There have been several innovations (such as those listed above) during the last few years which have materially altered the conditions under which private institutions must operate. These changes are so fundamentally significant that at this time it is not clear whether these colleges and universities can survive them without losing some of their characteristic independence and their pioneering and scholarly qualities. And, finally, he agrees that the laymen on the board are the people who should give strong leadership in the days ahead. The control of higher education in the United States, is largely vested in the hands of laymen, not in the hands of public officials or of professional educators. This is one of the distinctive characteristics of higher education in America. It is important that the laymen in education have a sufficiently clear understanding of educational trends, enough vision, courage and conviction to help guide or change these trends.

DOCUMENTATION AND COMMENTARY

[1] Robert Duncan, *College Trustees, Fund Raising and Public Relations*, Washington: American Alumni Council, 1960, p. 12.

[2] Harold Dodds, *The Academic President—Educator or Caretaker*, New York: McGraw-Hill Book Co., 1962, p. 221.

[3] Eduard C. Lindeman, "Why Education for Board Members?" Foreword to Charlotte K. Demarest, *The Board Member's Manual*, New York: National Publicity Council, 1951.

[4] Elisha Andrews, "The Organization of the University and the Distribution of Authority and Function Therein", National Association of State Universities Proceedings, 1907, p. 114.

[5] James McKeen Cattell, "Concerning the American University", *Popular Science Monthly*, June, 1902, p. 405.

[6] The University of Chicago, New York University, University of Miami, University of Houston, Boston University.

[7] David Hill, "Control of Tax-Supported Higher Education in the United States", New York: Carnegie Foundation for the Advancement of Teaching, 1934, p. 13.

[8] Rt. Rev. Alfred Horrigan, "The President and His Office", *Problems of Administration in the American College*, Washington: Catholic University of America Press, 1956, p. 14.

[9] Homer P. Rainey, "How Shall We Control Our Universities?", *Journal of Higher Education*, October, 1960, p. 17.

[10] Seymour E. Harris, "Introduction—Some Broad Issues", in *Higher Education in the United States* (Edited by Seymour E. Harris), Cambridge, Massachusetts: Harvard University Press, 1960, p. 18.

[11] John J. Corson, *Governance of Colleges and Universities*, New York: McGraw-Hill Book Company, 1960, p. 130.

[12] William H. Cowley, "Academic Government", *The Educational Forum*, January, 1951, p. 157.

[13] Hubert P. Beck, *Men Who Control Our Universities*, New York: King's County Press, 1947, p. 151.

[14] William H. Cowley, "The College President as a Leader", *Association of American College Bulletin*, December 1939, p. 546.

[15] Kenneth G. Patrick, "Three Basic Points", *Pride*, April 1961, p. 7.

[16] Glen Lloyd, "Blue Print for Trustees", *The University of Chicago Magazine*, Spring 1960, p. 10.

12 THE FUTURE OF HIGHER EDUCATION

There are several major factors extant in higher education which offer identifiable implications for the future of colleges and universities in this nation. The majority of these factors and implications bear directly upon the role of the trustee. Relating the role of the trustee or regent to these implications, and examining identifiable trends connected thereto, will be the function of this chapter.

PRESIDENTIAL WORKLOAD

The first implication to be considered among the principal issues in higher education is that of the burden of the presidency. Cause and effect relationships are seldom more apparent in college and university work than in this area.

Simply stated, the duties of the president have become so numerous and so complex that the position has in many cases become untenable. Long before inflation, depression, and other financial problems began to plague university presidents, some thoughtful people were questioning the effectiveness and efficiency of their higher institutions. These questions were raised, in the main, on the basis of the nearly impossible workload forcing able presidents out of the presidency. Wriston says, "The range of activity that may properly be called the function of a president has become so vast that no man can discharge all the duties that could reasonably be assigned to the office."[1] Although there are now vice presidents, deans, and presidential assistants available in most institutions, in many instances the delegation of authority has not occurred.

In addition to the problem of a heavy workload, many presidents are not qualified for the job temperamentally or professionally, thus compounding the difficulties of the presidency. As Benezet candidly observed, "There are really very few good presidents."[2] If this is true, steps should be taken by trustees to select presidents better qualified for the position; and if the workload is too great, concerted effort should be made to lighten the presidential schedule.

Another approach to the problem of overworked and undertrained presidents is for the trustees, with the help of faculty members and administrators, to develop a system of identifying, selecting and securing appropriate in-service training opportunities for their presidents. Only a small percentage of our college presidents have taken a preliminary or in-service course to qualify them for the position. It appears that ability to superintend educational work has not been regarded in all cases as the essential prerequisite. Actually, the head of the university should be one who has studied the educational problem from all sides; not necessarily a great scholar in any one department.

There is a discernible trend in the field that offers great promise for the solution of this problem of the wearing out of top administrators. Briefly stated, it is that many enlightened trustees recognize the problem and are pooling their knowledge and wisdom, effort and finances to solve it. Specifically, they are familiar with the restrictions and problems that surround the presidency, and they are taking steps to minimize them. These steps include the granting of more authority to the president, the securing of better qualified administrators to assist the president, and the providing of greater trustee support to the president.

Too many presidents have a "do-it-myself" attitude, possibly due to the shortage of well-qualified second and third echelon administrators. This problem has been recognized by foundations and universities, and there are some indications of progress being made to correct the situation. Many institutions, such as Teachers College (Columbia University), Harvard University and New York University, are offering courses and seminars in the administration of higher education. Many professional organizations (such as the American Council on Education, the Association of American Colleges and the Council for Financial Aid to Education) are offering publications and conferences that provide in-service training of considerable value to neophyte administrators. Through these and other efforts it is expected that eventually the supply of qualified administrators will catch up with the demand.

FACULTY REMUNERATION

The second implication to be considered among the central elements for higher education in the future is that of raising the salary and fringe benefits of faculty members. Minutes of board meetings indicate that trustees have (especially in the last few years) awakened to the fact that their faculties have been subsidizing their institutions by a willingness to accept totally inadequate remuneration. Fortunately, the pendulum is beginning to swing in the opposite direction and faculty salaries are starting to rise. Based upon research studies conducted by the American Association of University Professors, the American Alumni Council, the U. S. Office of Education and the Council for Financial Aid to Education, it seems safe to say that increased faculty remuneration is a definite trend for the future of higher education.

A clearly discernible trend with which trustees are concerned is that of effecting internal economies on campus in order that faculty salaries can continue to rise. It is not enough that external efforts to raise funds for faculty salaries be successful and continuous. There is an obvious and important relationship between the extent of institutional economies, especially in the area of logical curriculum expansion, and the extent to which salaries can be increased.[3] This is a controversial point upon which it is difficult to secure agreement. It is unlikely that anyone would object to the notion that unlimited curriculum expansion poses a threat to faculty salaries. However, the argument appears to revolve around what is meant by "logical" curriculum expansion. Curriculum expansion should be limited to those academic offerings that fulfill the stated educational program of the institution. Obviously, size of faculty, numbers of interested students, tradition of academic offerings, customary class size and availability of funds have a bearing on this matter.

Faculty remuneration is a policy matter which holds implications for the future role of trustees. This matter of faculty salary ranges involves the formulation of appropriate fiscal policy and the encouragement of vigorous administrative leadership to get and keep faculty salaries at a reasonably high level. This can be done in many ways, but there are two that warrant special mention at this point: First, the board must make certain that the regular income of the institution is such that it can meet normal salary expenses without undue strain; second, trustees, working with administration and faculty, must effect internal economies that will preclude any waste or unnecessary expenditures that would adversely affect faculty salaries.

The largest and most successful promotional programs are based upon an appeal for designated (or unrestricted) funds *for faculty salaries.*[4] This is not a new kind of appeal, but one that has been traced back about twenty years and may continue to be effective until remuneration for faculty members achieves parity with remuneration in other professional fields.

Coombs has noted that there is still a shortage of well qualified college teachers and that the salary situation is a causative factor. He says that, "A substantial rise in faculty compensation, relative to competing occupations, is certainly a prerequisite to correcting this imbalance. It is encouraging that, after a long period of erosion, faculty salaries have been rising at a fairly rapid pace."[5] In spite of the modest rise in teachers' salaries, the inevitable result of shortage, it is doubtful if colleges and universities will ever be in a financial position to outbid industry and research institutions.

CURRICULAR PROBLEMS

An implication impinging upon the future of higher education is the serious situation surrounding the curriculum in most colleges and universities. As indicated in preceding portions of this study, while not intimately involved with curriculum of its college or university, the board must assume ultimate responsibility for the academic program. There are various shades of opinion as to how closely trustees (or even the president) should be related to this most important aspect of the institution's operations. For example, some trustees interviewed indicated that there should be a "hands off" policy for board members; others went so far as to suggest that the trustees should be involved actively in curriculum matters at the policy level; none wanted to "take back" the curriculum in the Ruml sense.

I concur with the conclusions of several distinguished researchers, that academic programs have grown so enormously and so chaotically in most institutions that the faculty (and the administration earlier) has seemingly lost control of the process of adding new courses. Commenting on this problem, Hester says, "At the college level we frequently encounter the problem of having to give weight to subjects simply because the individuals who represent them must be treated with respect. As a result, many curricula are based upon compromises among competing claims of subject matter specialists. This is partly a consequence of the right of college faculties to determine the curriculum, a situation which can result in horse trading. It is also a disappointing commentary on the ability of some college administrators to exert strong curricular leadership."[6]

This burgeoning of the curriculum constitutes one of the most serious problems in higher education today. While many educators agree with this premise, there are some who strongly disagree.[7] There is a general acceptance, however, of the notion that some new device is needed to provide strong academic leadership in solving this problem. Two of the difficulties in this matter are, first, the relatively complete separation of academic decision making by the faculty from financial decision making by the president and trustees; second, the lack of programming of academic decisions is attributable to the insistence of the professor upon self-direction.

It seems reasonable that certain difficulties would arise in any organization or enterprise where the decision making for program matters was separated from the decision making for financial matters. Colleges and universities are hardly exceptions to the rule. For that reason, it would seem desirable to avoid the difficulties by bringing the program and financial functions more closely together. The second point is logical in that teachers and professors usually operate as individuals on nearly an autonomous basis. The individuality of their teaching sets them more apart from their colleagues than is the case in other occupations. Partially in consequence of these characteristics, faculty members as a group encounter some difficulties in handling objectively decision making with respect to the curriculum.

From what has been said and documented in earlier portions of this study it appears that one of the implications for trustees in the future of higher education may be their more extensive involvement in curricular matters. If properly oriented and introduced to the academic program, trustees can be of great value in formulating policies both wise and just.

One of the problems that must be faced is that trustees will need considerable orientation to and experience with curricular matters before they are able to prescribe reform in this area. One of the advantages trustees may possess at the outset of their term on a board is their objectivity or disinterestedness in partisan politics and departmental attempts to achieve greater size, power and prestige.

Eddy says that far too many faculty members and administrators cling to tradition and ignore new departures and dimensions in higher education. He points out that, "Vested interests on every campus prevent recognition of the obvious. Established customs, long-standing departmental and administrative structure, and sentimentalized traditions ... keep the colleges from responding with the vigor and enthusiasm of the new students. The interests of the youngster who is ready for something new in the way of learning is quickly dampened by the self-oriented faculty member who sees a threat in change and resists it out of apprehension."[8] It is clear that trustees can help by offering guidance on new curricular adjuncts because they are more active in the business, civic and social life of the local and national community than the campus-centered faculty, and, thus, are in a position to see what kind of *new* knowledge and *different* skills are needed in the community. This would apply particularly to university trustees of institutions where graduate and professional education and training are offered.

Faculties like to describe the role of the college president as *primus inter pares* or *non dominus sed dux.* This favorite pastime of "leveling off" the chief executive officer may, in some cases, be needed and desired. However, as admitted by trustees, administrators and even teachers, it sometimes tends to remove the president from the moral authority which is frequently more essential than legal authority for decision making in academic affairs. The ironic twist to the matter is that faculty members hurt themselves (both financially and professionally) more than any other group when they deprive their leader of his right to lead. Here indeed is an area for forthright trustee action in the days ahead.

STUDENT ENROLLMENT

The fourth dominant factor affecting the future of higher education is the accelerated expansion of student enrollments. Innumerable studies have been conducted and reports published on this subject in the last several years. The purpose of this section is to suggest a role and relationship that college and university trustees might have in the face of enormously increasing enrollments.

The U. S. Office of Education reports that about 5½ million students are attending institutions of higher education in 1966 and that this figure may double by 1980. This magnitude of increase constitutes a serious problem for administrators; a problem with which trustees should become familiar and with which they should assist in solving.[9] Normal institutional growth is a simple administrative matter, but growth of the kind envisioned for the next several years requires careful evaluation and the formulation of new policies regarding admissions, retentions and expansion. In concert with senior faculty members and key administrators, trustees should provide some consultation and advice on how to cope with problems arising in this area. (See Appendix D.)

There are several reasons for trustee involvement in this matter of expansion. First, being an off-campus group, trustees represent the general public. The public must be served, even by the private institutions, and the trustees should help articulate what service is needed. Secondly, trustees hold the charter of the institution and are responsible for maintaining (if not increasing) the institution's academic reputation in spite of vastly expanded numbers of students. Thirdly, whether the institution is publicly or privately supported, trustees in large measure influence the finances that must be raised or appropriated to meet the increased costs of swollen enrollments. Fourthly, the board is a "court of last appeal" and as such trustees may have to arbitrate when the inevitable controversy arises as to what schools, departments, or courses will be added or expanded to cope with the impending tidal wave of students.[10]

INSTITUTIONAL FINANCE

The fifth salient example of an implication affecting the future of colleges and universities is that of monetary support. There is no area of the institution's operation as close to the trustee's function and responsibility as that of finance. That institutional finance will continue as a paramount concern of boards of trustees is unanimously accepted by the key trustees interviewed. What is investigated here is the proposition that this particular concern (adequate financing) will become intensified in the next few years. Evidence at hand indicates that more and more institutions (such as individual colleges and universities) and groups of institutions (such as the state associations of colleges) are asking their trustees to assume greater responsibility and authority for the raising of money.[11]

This important trustee function is not limited to the privately-supported institution. Tax-supported colleges and universities are mobilizing their trustees to take their "case" (the need for more money) to the legislature via the public. In several states, (e.g., Oregon, New Mexico and New York) the public colleges and universities have been brought together under a single board of trustees or regents to enhance their financial positions. In many instances, the public institutions have hired professional fund-raising firms and organized their trustees, alumni and friends to solicit gifts from the private sectors of the economy.

Key trustees and experienced educational leaders, even those from public institutions, take a dim view of this latter action. The feeling predominates that, while most tax-supported institutions could use more funds than they are currently receiving, they are far better off than most privately-supported institutions, and the former should not actively compete with the latter for the limited private sector funds that are available.[12]

Trustees of privately-supported colleges and universities, from the largest and richest to the smallest and poorest, have a difficult and important task. There is the primary responsibility of seeing to it that the financial operations of the institution keep up with its needs. Although they are concerned wih internal efficiency and economy, their major financial concern is raising money externally.

There are several factors that make necessary the raising of money by the private colleges and universities. Until recently few, if any, institutions charged the students what it cost to educate them; as enrollments at low tuition figures grew, so too did the deficits; following World War II, inflation curbed the value of the dollar, and yet costs of services and materials spiraled.

There are several reasons why trustees are better fundraisers than other college-connected groups. Trustees are usually persons of means and can contribute generously themselves; they are usually well-connected in the community and can secure substantial gifts from friends and business colleagues; by tradition they assume greater responsibility for the proper financing of the institution than do the administrators, faculty, or alumni.

INSTITUTIONAL IMAGE

The sixth critical area portending a trend for the future of higher education is the so-called "image" problem in colleges and universities. The image is alleged to be the conception of the institution held by its various publics. With greater frequency, trustees and regents are playing a vigorous role in shaping the public's thinking about particular institutions. Where in the past the only publicity a trustee usually received was mention in the college catalogue, trustees are now increasingly identified with their institutions.

As the need for public understanding and support of higher education increases, so, too, must increase the public relations activities of the board members. They are the people well known and (usually) well respected by their peers in the community. Not being on the payroll, they are considered more objective than administrators or faculty members when they speak of and for the institution. As observed by Pollard, they are usually civic or business leaders in their areas, whereas most administrators and faculty members are more campus-bound and not usually opinion makers in the community.[13]

For these reasons, trustees in the past decade played an important role in molding the image of their institutions. It appears that this role must be increased further if the institutions are to secure the understanding and support they need. There are many thoughtful leaders in our society who feel that the future of higher education in America will depend in large measure on the effectiveness of the lay leaders—the trustees and regents—connected with our institutions.[14] Of this, there can be little doubt.

FUTURE POSSIBILITIES

The final portion of this chapter deals with futures. These are futures primarily for institutions of higher education with particular reference to the emergent role of the trustee.

As mentioned above, there are those (such as trustees and presidents interviewed) who feel the future of our colleges and universities, both public and private, will be secure and productive in *direct proportion* to the amount of dedicated service the trustees give these institutions.

The foregoing pages have analyzed, described and documented six areas that hold distinct and important implications bearing upon the historical, current and possible future role of the trustees. Evidence presented in earlier pages clarifies and qualifies the thesis that the trustees have played an important part in higher education in the past, and may be destined to play a somewhat different and even more important part in the future.

It is no simple task to define all the trends which would seem to indicate what the future of higher education and college trustees will be. However, it is possible to offer some prescription as to the generalized role of the college trustee in the days ahead:

1. Trustees will be more carefully selected and more adequately oriented.
2. Trustees will be assuming greater authority and responsibility.
3. Trustees will give more generously of their time, talents and money.
4. Trustees will concern themselves with internal economies as well as external fund-raising.
5. Trustees will select and elect better qualified presidents who are men of learning *and* management.
6. Trustees will empower and encourage presidents to exert stronger leadership, especially in curricular matters.

In Academe, as in other facets of our society, the pressures of today will determine the priorities established for tomorrow. Trustees should be cognizant of the three primary pressures unique to this age. From these three—unprecedented growth in *enrollment,* in *knowledge,* and in *federal involvement*—all others seem to flow. Before these pressures can be dealt with properly, and before institutional priorities and programs can be established, there must be a philosophical context embodying a logical statement of institutional goals and objectives. This philosophy and its expression will in the future increasingly become the responsibility of enlightened trustees in higher education.

DOCUMENTATION AND COMMENTARY

[1] Henry M. Wriston, "The Future of the College Presidency: Some Serio-Comic Observations on the Head Man and His Maneuvers", *College and University Business*, November 1954, pp. 30, 31.

[2] Louis T. Benezet, "The Office of the President", Gerald P. Burns (Ed.), *Administrators in Higher Education*, New York: Harper and Row, 1962, p. 120.

[3] Earl J. McGrath, *Memo to a College Faculty Member*, New York: Columbia University, 1961, p. 15.

[4] Susan Auslander, *A Report of Stewardship*, New York: Independent College Funds of America, Inc., 1962.

[5] Philip Coombs in Dexter M. Keezer, (Ed.), *Financing Higher Education 1960-70*, New York: McGraw-Hill Book Co., 1959, p. 19.

[6] James M. Hester, from an address delivered to the special studies and elementary school teachers, Garden City Public Schools, September 5, 1961.

[7] Douglas J. Brown, "Mr. Ruml's Memo: A Wrong Approach to the Right Problem", *The Journal of Higher Education*, Columbus, Vol. XXX, No. 8, November 1959, p. 413.

[8] Edward D. Eddy, Jr., "The New Student in the Old College", *School and Society*, New York, Vol. 90, No. 2207, March 24, 1962, p. 135.

[9] E. C. Elliot, M. M. Chambers and W. A. Ashbrook, *The Government of Higher Education*, New York: American Book Co., 1935, p. 137.

[10] Raymond Hughes, *A Manual for Trustees*, Ames: The Iowa State College Press, 1943, p. 48.

[11] Louis T. Benezet, "Report of the Chairman", New York: Independent College Funds of America, Inc., January, 1962.

[12] Phyllis Michelfelder, *Blueprint 1960-70*, New York: Independent College Funds of America, Inc., 1960, pp. 1-16.

[13] John Pollard, *Fund-Raising for Higher Education*, New York: Harper and Brothers, 1958, p. 56.

[14] Louis T. Benezet, in a speech to the annual meeting of the Association of American Colleges, Boston, January 12, 1960.

APPENDIX A

While most scholars of and practitioners in the field of college administration agree that there is a paucity of research and writing on the trusteeship, within the past decade several excellent books have been published. Since much of the foregoing study has been based upon these earlier volumes, it seems desirable to list and annotate some of these for further reference.

Brubacher, John S. and Willis Rudy, *Higher Education in Transition*, New York: Harper and Brothers, 1958. This study clarifies the problems of the present by means of perspectives on the past. It is designed for persons interested in ideas, ideals and traditions. It is valuable as a reference book for scholars of the field of higher education.

Corson, John J., *Governance of Colleges and Universities*, New York: McGraw-Hill, 1960. This is a book about how higher educational institutions are directed by their boards and administered by their officers. It emphasizes the necessary cooperation that must be achieved in operations between trustees, administrators, faculty and students. An excellent book for trustees.

Henderson, Algo D., *Policies and Practices in Higher Education*, New York: Harper & Brothers, 1960. This work deals with the problems and potentialities facing colleges and universities. It is concerned with contemporary, rather than past or future happenings in higher education. A splendid book for administrators.

Martorana, S. V., *College Boards of Trustees*, Washington, D. C.: The Center for Applied Research in Education, Inc.,

1963. This study presents the most up-to-date consideration of how and why boards of trustees or regents function in behalf of their colleges and universities. Because of its size (104 pages), it tends to summarize in places where greater detail would be highly worthwhile.

Rauh, Morton A., *College and University Trusteeship*, Yellow Springs, Ohio: The Antioch Press, 1959. This is a book that offers a compilation of ideas and experience garnered from twenty-two board chairmen and distilled by an able administrator. It utilizes the modified case study method of analysis of problems facing trustees. Hardly a scholarly document, but a handy "Handbook" for collateral reading.

Ruml, Beardsley and Donald H. Morrison, *Memo to a College Trustee*, New York, N. Y.: McGraw-Hill, 1959. This book offers some challenging new ideas on how the trustees should exercise greater leadership in the actual operation of their institutions. It is interesting reading for all persons in higher education. A highly controversial, but significant book to be read with one's critical faculties always on the alert.

APPENDIX B

The following distinguished trustees served as advisors—a kind of sounding board—for parts of this study:

Mr. Brooke Alexander (Mt. Holyoke College), Assistant to the Publisher, Fortune Magazine, New York, New York

Mr. Laird Bell (University of Chicago), Senior Partner, Bell, Boyd, Marshall and Lloyd, Chicago, Illinois

Mrs. Norman Chandler (University of California), Vice President, Los Angeles Times, Los Angeles, California

Mr. Charles Holloway (Oregon State Board of Higher Education), Vice President, Northwest Natural Gas Company, Portland, Oregon

Mr. Frank Jenks (Loyola University), Retired Chairman and President, International Harvester Company, Chicago, Illinois

Mr. Clarence J. Myers (Colgate University), Retired President, New York Life Insurance Company, New York, New York

Mr. Kenneth G. Patrick (Mills College of Education), Vice President, Council for Financial Aid to Education, New York, New York

Mr. Frederick Patterson (Tuskegee Institute), President, United Negro College Fund, New York, New York

Mr. Ordway Tead (New York City Board of Higher Education), Former Vice President, Harper & Row, New York, New York

Mr. Homer Wadsworth (Parke College), Executive Director, Kansas City Association of Trusts, Kansas City, Missouri

In addition to serving more than 500 private institutions as trustees-at-large of the Independent College Funds of America, several of these business leaders are board members of individual colleges or universities as indicated. They have given graciously of their time and talents to this study.

Mr. George Champion (Tuskegee Institute), Chairman, The Chase Manhattan Bank, New York, New York

Mr. Gilbert W. Chapman, Retired President, The Yale & Towne Manufacturing Company, New York, New York

Mr. Byron K. Elliott (Northeastern University), Chairman, John Hancock Mutual Life Insurance Company, Boston, Massachusetts

Mr. Roger S. Firestone (Lincoln University), President, Firestone Plastics Company, Pottstown, Pennsylvania

Mr. J. Simon Fluor (Chapman College), Chairman, Fluor Corporation, Ltd., Los Angeles, California

Mr. Edward P. Hamilton (Lawrence College), Chairman, Hamilton Manufacturing Company, Two Rivers, Wisconsin

Mr. Grover M. Hermann (Illinois Institute of Technology), Honorary Chairman, Martin-Marietta Corporation, Chicago, Illinois

Mr. Stanley deJ. Osborne, Partner, Lazard Freres & Company, New York, New York

Mr. Stuart T. Saunders (Rollins College), Chairman, Pennsylvania Railroad Company, Philadelphia, Pennsylvania

Mr. James M. VerMeulen, President, American Seating Company, Grand Rapids, Michigan

Mr. Herbert Willetts, Retired President, Socony Mobil Oil Company, New York, New York

APPENDIX C

Trustees and regents should be familiar with salary schedules in their own institutions and with the national aver-
ages. As competition becomes keener for qualified faculty
and administrators, it is incumbent upon board members
to assist the president in developing remunerative induce-
ments that will attract and retain the desired personnel.

FIGURE I
MEDIAN SALARIES FOR NINE MONTHS OF FULL-TIME TEACHING, 1961-62 AND 1963-64

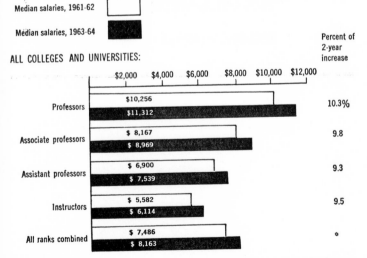

Median salaries, 1961-62

Median salaries, 1963-64

Percent of
2-year
increase

ALL COLLEGES AND UNIVERSITIES:

$2,000 $4,000 $6,000 $8,000 $10,000 $12,000

Professors $10,256 / $11,312 — 10.3%

Associate professors $ 8,167 / $ 8,969 — 9.8

Assistant professors $ 6,900 / $ 7,539 — 9.3

Instructors $ 5,582 / $ 6,114 — 9.5

All ranks combined $ 7,486 / $ 8,163 — *

*Since median rather than average salary is shown here, the percent of increase for combined groups
is not computed.

177

FIGURE I (Cont.)

ALL RANKS BY TYPE OF INSTITUTION:

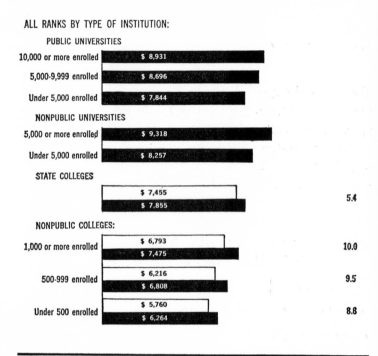

PUBLIC UNIVERSITIES

10,000 or more enrolled $ 8,931

5,000-9,999 enrolled $ 8,696

Under 5,000 enrolled $ 7,844

NONPUBLIC UNIVERSITIES

5,000 or more enrolled $ 9,318

Under 5,000 enrolled $ 8,257

STATE COLLEGES

$ 7,455

$ 7,855   5.4

NONPUBLIC COLLEGES:

1,000 or more enrolled $ 6,793
                          $ 7,475   10.0

500-999 enrolled $ 6,216
                    $ 6,808   9.5

Under 500 enrolled $ 5,760
                      $ 6,264   8.8

FIGURE II
MEDIAN SALARIES OF CERTAIN ADMINISTRATIVE OFFICERS IN COLLEGES AND UNIVERSITIES, 1961-62 AND 1963-64

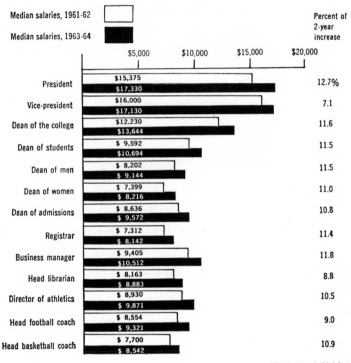

	Median salaries, 1961-62	Median salaries, 1963-64	Percent of 2-year increase
President	$15,375	$17,330	12.7%
Vice-president	$16,000	$17,130	7.1
Dean of the college	$12,230	$13,644	11.6
Dean of students	$ 9,592	$10,694	11.5
Dean of men	$ 8,202	$ 9,144	11.5
Dean of women	$ 7,399	$ 8,216	11.0
Dean of admissions	$ 8,636	$ 9,572	10.8
Registrar	$ 7,312	$ 8,142	11.4
Business manager	$ 9,405	$10,512	11.8
Head librarian	$ 8,163	$ 8,883	8.8
Director of athletics	$ 8,930	$ 9,871	10.5
Head football coach	$ 8,554	$ 9,321	9.0
Head basketball coach	$ 7,700	$ 8,542	10.9

NEA Research Division

FIGURE III
MEDIAN SALARIES FOR NINE MONTHS OF FULL-TIME
TEACHING, 1961-62 AND 1963-64

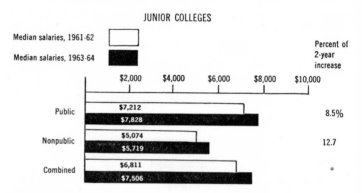

JUNIOR COLLEGES

Median salaries, 1961-62

Median salaries, 1963-64

Percent of
2-year
increase

	$2,000	$4,000	$6,000	$8,000	$10,000	
Public	$7,212					8.5%
	$7,828					
Nonpublic	$5,074					12.7
	$5,719					
Combined	$6,811					*
	$7,506					

*Since median rather than average salary is shown here, the percent of increase for combined groups
is not computed.

The bar graphs above provide a clear and current picture of this rather complicated matter of college and university salaries. They are included through the courtesy
of the Research Division of the National Education Association.

APPENDIX D

Many trustees and regents are acutely aware of the problems of space utilization faced by their institutions in coping with the oncoming student explosion. However, not all board members are aware of the differential existing between enrollment growth in public as compared to private institutions.

THE COMING BOOM IN COLLEGE ENROLLMENTS

The number of students will increase threefold. . .

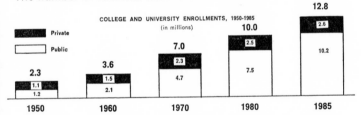

. . . but the proportion in private institutions will drop sharply

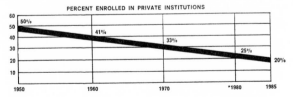

Source: "Letter to a College President," by Sidney G. Tickton, Fund for the Advancement of Education, 1963

WHY ENROLLMENTS WILL RISE TO NEW HIGHS

There will be more young people of college age. . .

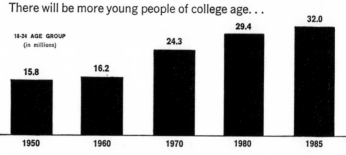

18-24 AGE GROUP
(in millions)

1950	1960	1970	1980	1985
15.8	16.2	24.3	29.4	32.0

. . . and a larger proportion of them will be in college

PERCENT OF 18-24 AGE GROUP ATTENDING COLLEGE

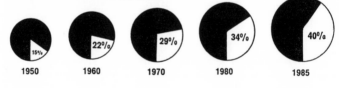

1950	1960	1970	1980	1985
15%	22%	29%	34%	40%

Enrollments are rising because of three major factors and several minor factors. Among the major factors are (1) there are more college age people extant, (2) a larger percentage of people want a college education, and (3) automation and other technical advances decrease job opportunities available to young people.

The above graphs are reproduced from "Letter to a College President," by Sidney G. Tickton, with the permission of the publisher, The Fund for the Advancement of Education.

APPENDIX E

The graph below indicates the percentage sharing of financial support by the various sources of income utilized in financing higher education.

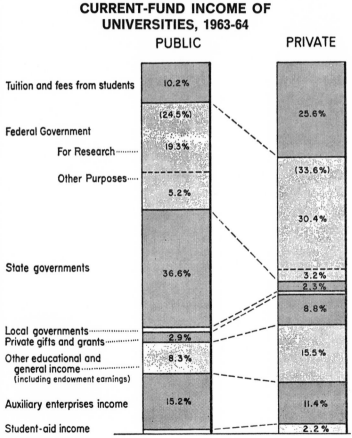

CURRENT-FUND INCOME OF UNIVERSITIES, 1963-64

	PUBLIC	PRIVATE
Tuition and fees from students	10.2%	25.6%
Federal Government	(24.5%)	(33.6%)
For Research	19.3%	30.4%
Other Purposes	5.2%	
State governments	36.6%	3.2%
		2.3%
		8.8%
Local governments	2.9%	
Private gifts and grants		15.5%
Other educational and general income (including endowment earnings)	8.3%	
Auxiliary enterprises income	15.2%	11.4%
Student-aid income		2.2%

Source U.S. Office of Education

INDEX